SCOTTISH BORD...
JEDBURGH GRAMMAR SCHOOL
HIGH STREET
JEDBURGH
TD8 6DQ

Raising Boys' Achievement

Jon Pickering

Published by Network Educational Press Ltd.
PO Box 635
Stafford
ST16 1BF

First Published 1997
Reprinted 1999, 2001
© Jon Pickering 1997

ISBN 1 85539 040 X

Jon Pickering asserts the moral right to be identified
as the author of this work

All rights reserved. No part of this publication may be
reproduced, stored in a retrieval system or reproduced or
transmitted in any form or by any other means, electronic,
mechanical, photocopying (with the exception of page 18)
recording or otherwise without the prior written
permission of the Publisher. This book may not be lent, resold,
hired out or otherwise disposed of by way of trade in any
form of binding or cover other than that in which it is
published, without the prior consent of the Publisher.

Every effort has been made to contact copyright holders and the
publishers apologise for any omissions, which they will be
pleased to rectify at the earliest opportunity.

Crown copyright is reproduced with the permission of the
Controller of Her Majesty's Stationery Office.

Templates on pages 51 and 52 by permission of Geoff Hannan.

Series Editor - Professor Tim Brighouse
Edited by Chris Griffin
Design & layout by Neil Hawkins, NEP
Illustrations by Joe Rice

Printed in Great Britain by
MPG Books Ltd., Bodmin, Cornwall

Acknowledgments

This book is dedicated to Barbara, David and Grace for their support and inspiration.

Thanks to Paul Hamm who started it all.

Thanks to Michael Barber, Caroline Lodge, Kate Myers and Louise Stoll for their encouragement throughout.

Thanks to my editor Chris Griffin, for his hard work, patience, good humour and kind words.

And thanks to all the boys who inspired and contributed to the activities and ideas in the book.

Jon Pickering
May, 1997

Foreword

A teacher's task is much more ambitious than it used to be and demands a focus on the subtleties of teaching and learning and on the emerging knowledge of school improvement.

This is what this series is about.

Teaching can be a very lonely activity. The time honoured practice of a single teacher working alone in the classroom is still the norm; yet to operate alone is, in the end, to become isolated and impoverished. This series addresses two issues – the need to focus on practical and useful ideas connected with teaching and learning and the wish thereby to provide some sort of an antidote to the loneliness of the long distance teacher who is daily berated by an anxious society.

Teachers flourish best when, in key stage teams or departments (or more rarely whole schools), their talk is predominantly about teaching and learning and where, unconnected with appraisal, they are privileged to observe each other teach; to plan and review their work together; and to practise the habit of learning from each other new teaching techniques. But how does this state of affairs arise? Is it to do with the way staffrooms are physically organised so that the walls bear testimony to interesting articles and in the corner there is a dedicated computer tuned to 'conferences' about SEN, school improvement, the teaching of English etc., and whether, in consequence, the teacher leaning over the shoulder of the enthusiastic IT colleagues sees the promise of interesting practice elsewhere? Has the primary school cracked it when it organises successive staff meetings in different classrooms and invites the 'host' teacher to start the meeting with a 15 minute exposition of their classroom organisation and management? Or is it the same staff sharing, on a rota basis, a slot on successive staff meeting agenda when each in turn reviews a new book they have used with their class? And what of the whole school which now uses 'active' and 'passive' concerts of carefully chosen music as part of their accelerated learning techniques?

It is of course well understood that even excellent teachers feel threatened when first they are observed. Hence the epidemic of trauma associated with OFSTED. The constant observation of the teacher in training seems like that of the learner driver. Once you have passed your test and can drive unaccompanied, you do. You often make lots of mistakes and sometimes get into bad habits. Woe betide, however, the back seat driver who tells you so. In the same way the new teacher quickly loses the habit of observing others and being observed. So how do we get a confident, mutual observation debate going? One school I know found a simple and therefore brilliant solution. The Head of the History Department asked that a young colleague plan lessons for her – the Head of Department – to teach. This lesson she then taught, and was observed by the young colleague. There was subsequent discussion, in which the young teacher asked,

> *"Why did you divert the question and answer session I had planned?"*
> *and was answered by,*
> *"Because I could see that I needed to arrest the attention of the group by the window with some "hands-on" role play, etc."*

This lasted an hour and led to a once-a-term repeat discussion which, in the end, was adopted by the whole school. The whole school subsequently changed the pattern of its meetings to consolidate extended debate about teaching and learning. The two teachers claimed that because one planned and the other taught both were implicated but neither alone was responsible or felt 'got at'.

So there are practices which are both practical and more likely to make teaching a rewarding and successful activity. They can, as it were, increase the likelihood of a teacher surprising the pupils into understanding or doing something they did not think they could do rather than simply entertaining them or worse still occupying them. There are ways of helping teachers judge the best method of getting pupil expectation just ahead of self-esteem.

This series focuses on straightforward interventions which individual schools and teachers use to make life more rewarding for themselves and those they teach. Teachers deserve nothing less, for they are the architects of tomorrow's society, and society's ambition for what they achieve increases as each year passes.

Professor Tim Brighouse.

Contents

INTRODUCTION

How can schools raise boys' achievement?

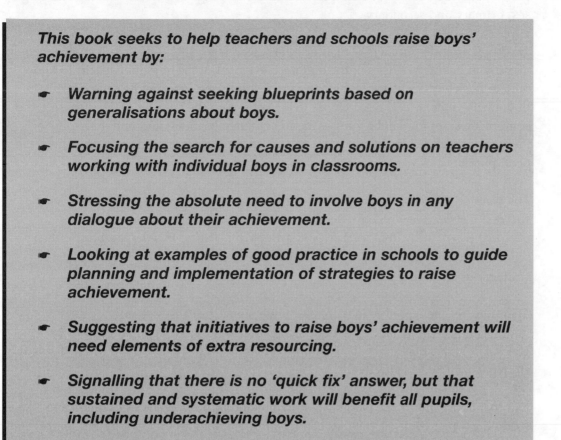

This book seeks to help teachers and schools raise boys' achievement by:

- ☞ *Warning against seeking blueprints based on generalisations about boys.*

- ☞ *Focusing the search for causes and solutions on teachers working with individual boys in classrooms.*

- ☞ *Stressing the absolute need to involve boys in any dialogue about their achievement.*

- ☞ *Looking at examples of good practice in schools to guide planning and implementation of strategies to raise achievement.*

- ☞ *Suggesting that initiatives to raise boys' achievement will need elements of extra resourcing.*

- ☞ *Signalling that there is no 'quick fix' answer, but that sustained and systematic work will benefit all pupils, including underachieving boys.*

Raising boys' achievement is an issue in many schools, largely because there is a widespread perception that boys are underachieving at all ages and at all stages of their schooling. Much of the high-profile debate about boys' underachievement has been highly charged and largely negative. It has essentially focused on the failure of boys in comparison with girls, and has frequently placed the blame for this failure on boys' attitudes to school.

Under Pressure

The Guardian 11.3.96. Grant L (© The Guardian)

Words of Comfort for males
Boys are under-achieving
What can we do?

TES 22.03.96, Barton A (© Times Supplements Ltd, 1997)

Anti-School bias 'blights boys for life'

The Times 06.03.96, O'Leary J & Charter D (© Times Newspapers Ltd, 1996)

NOT WORKING

TES 15.03.96, (© Times Supplements Ltd, 1997)

This book encourages teachers to think positively about boys, and to do so by working with the boys in their schools. It does not provide easy answers or a general template for teachers to use as an easy way to raise boys' achievement. However, it does support teachers by opening up areas to explore, based on a combination of school-based research and a study of examples of good practice.

Research shows that it is possible to avoid, or reverse, the stereotypes which have led to boys being labelled as unwilling or uninterested learners. It shows that boys do want to learn and do well at school, but they often want to do so in a way which is challenging to the confidence and authority of teachers. Boys want to learn at all ages and in all phases, and the book gives examples of this from a range of schools – mixed and single sex, primary and secondary.

The book provides teachers with a series of research activities which will enable them to identify in detail the causes of the underachievement of the boys they teach. To know how to raise boys' achievement we have to research and identify the causes for their underachievement. This research has to be focused on the boys we teach. If it isn't, the solutions we opt for will be guesses based on generalisations, and will therefore be ineffective. For teachers in mixed-sex schools the strategies should raise the achievement of all pupils.

The running theme of the book is the 'uniqueness' of individual schools. Achieving successful strategies with boys depends almost exclusively on the work and personalities of individual teachers and groups of teachers. It is the teachers in their schools who have the knowledge, experience and expertise to decide on the best strategies for their boys.

Therefore, teachers need to look for and understand the causes of any underachievement by talking to underachieving boys in particular and pupils in general. It is this dialogue which results in effective strategies. Without the dialogue the strategies will be less effective.

External data can provide possible research methods, hints at strategies that have worked in other contexts, theories about learning, issues around gender influences, and suggestions about setting up small or large school-based projects. But teachers need to apply the methods to the context in which they work, in order to address the individual learning needs of the boys they teach and to reflect the uniqueness of their school.

All of the book's activities have been used in schools. They have been used:

- for whole school INSET days to either initiate or maintain developments
- by teachers in departments, key stage groups, pastoral and cross curricular teams
- by individual teachers in their own classrooms.

The book requires teachers to be persistent and rigorous in approach. Saying 'Done that' will not be enough. It is what we as teachers learn and develop that brings insight into what makes our individual boys successful learners. The work will never be complete, but it will be all the more rewarding for every gain made and every boy realising his true potential.

The book is in three parts.

Part One comprises a long section with six activities which provide readers with opportunities to reflect and work on some of the book's issues and approaches.

Part Two is divided into six sections. Each section looks closely at a specific aspect of boys' underachievement. These are *attitudes, peer group pressure, biological issues, school influence, equal opportunities* and *central government policy*. They are all connected to the underachievement of boys through their potential as identifiable causes of underachievement. Each section describes practical research activities and ends with a short case study.

Part Three invites readers to reflect on what they have learned anew or have adapted and refined from different parts of the book. They are encouraged to reflect on what they might do next for all pupils – including boys who are underachieving.

The book concludes with a *References, Recommended Reading and Useful Contacts* section.

How to use the book

- ☞ Read the brief introduction at the start of each section to get a feel of the contents and direction of that section.

- ☞ Get an idea of each section from the advanced organiser at the start.

- ☞ Try to do the activities first. Before you can think about possible solutions and the development of strategies, you need to understand the causes of the underachievement of the boys you teach yourself.

- ☞ Use the examples of good practice and research evidence to add an extra dimension to your thoughts.

- ☞ Discuss activities, findings, issues and concerns with colleagues (in your own school and in others).

- ☞ Use your boys (and their parents) to inform your thoughts. They are your most important resource – as potential partners, not just as informants.

- ☞ Look at the 'stimulus' quotations from writers on schools and consider reading their research for further insights.

- ☞ Review your thoughts by using the 'dos-and don'ts' summary at the end of Parts One and Two.

Of course, you can read the book through without doing the activities. This will start you thinking, help you to question and develop your own practice, and offer you solutions to consider. Alternatively, you might do some of the activities on a selective basis, choosing those which are more relevant to your context.

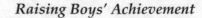

What do you know about Boys' Underachievement?

This section will ask you to examine closely what you know about boys' achievement in your school. This will be done through six specific activities designed to provide baseline evidence about your own school which will enable you to reflect on what needs to be done to raise the achievement of the boys.

The activities will help to develop an informed understanding of boys' achievement in your school. Setting off on strategies and solutions before some consideration of the 'real' state of boys' achievement may bring about some quick success, but this will be built on incomplete and shaky foundations. Like a building, the results may be quite impressive at first, but will soon start to show the cracks!

However, do not spend too long in reflective mode, as this can lead to inertia. Of course, you may find the activities develop a life of their own and take time to do thoroughly. If so, this will not be a problem, as long as it does not extend the reflection time too much. It is a question of getting the balance of reflection and activity right.

For teachers looking to raise the achievement of boys, the initial reflection must aim to establish the precise nature and scope of the problem in their school. Once done, strategies and activities can be developed which build on existing areas of success and address real concerns, rather than perceived problems.

Activity 1   Generalisations about Boys

Advanced Organiser

☛ *Focus on causes of boys' underachievement in your school.*

☛ *Compare your thoughts with colleagues, friends and family.*

☛ *Look for differences and similarities.*

☛ *Look for school-based and external factors.*

☛ *Compare your findings with national perceptions.*

☛ *Ask how what you find might help you adapt your practice.*

There are many suggested reasons for boys' underachievement. What do you think are the main causes for the underachievement of boys in your school? List five below in order of importance.

Causes of Boys' Underachievement

1...

2...

3...

4...

5...

When you have done this, ask one or two colleagues what they think are the main causes of boys' underachievement. You could also ask one or two friends or members of your family, so that you have a reasonable variety of responses. If possible, ask parents and a small number of pupils (both boys and girls if you work in a mixed-sex school.)

Try to categorise the response under headings such as *Boys' Attitudes, Employment Patterns* or *Literacy Problems*. Then ask yourself:

? **What are the similarities and differences between the responses?**

? **Are the perceived causes school-based or linked to external causes?**

? **Do some respondents indicate there is not a problem? What reasons do they give?**

? **Do the different 'groups' you asked show similar responses or not? If so, do they have common perceptions?**

? **Were any of the responses exactly the same?**

? **How many different categories of response did you come up with?**

? **Did you learn anything new? Were you surprised by (m)any of the responses?**

When you have finished this activity, you might want to look at the list of causes of boys' underachievement most commonly put forward in books, newspapers and on the television and radio in the last few years (see page 27).

? How do the lists compare?

? Is there any significance for your school in the similarities or the differences?

? Above all, how can the causes, singly or collectively, help you to raise achievement in your classroom?

Much of the debate about boys' underachievement has concentrated on causes outside classrooms. This has to be a matter of concern, as research into school effectiveness suggests that it is *inside the classroom* where schools make real differences to levels of achievement.

Stimulus Quotation 1

"A focus solely on external conditions diverts energy and attention from the circumstances within schools and classrooms that can have a positive impact on the experiences of students."

from Speaking Up: Students' Perspectives on Schools,
Phi Delta Kappan *Vol. 73 No. 9, Phelan P et al. (1992)*

It is important to remind ourselves that it is *individual teachers* who make the difference with pupils. Recent research shows that this appears to be particularly significant for many boys. The following activity asks teachers to consider what it is about teachers and teaching which makes the most impact on boys' learning.

Activity 2   Focusing on Teaching and Learning

Advanced Organiser

☞ **Are OFSTED's opinions about effective teaching similar to teachers'?**

☞ **Are pupils' opinions similar to teachers' and OFSTED's?**

☞ **Do boys and girls differ about which styles of teaching lead to effective learning?**

What makes an effective teacher?

The Office for Standards in Education (OFSTED) regards teaching as the major contributory factor to pupils' attainment, progress and response. In the 1995 *OFSTED Handbook*, judgements about the quality of teaching are based on eight characteristics of effective teaching.

Activity 2.1

Below are the OFSTED characteristics of effective teaching. Put them into rank order according to the extent to which you think they promote the learning of all pupils. If you think it is impossible to separate out individual characteristics, consider whether it is possible to divide them into three groups, namely (a) essential, (b) important, (c) not that important.

OFSTED CHARACTERISTICS OF EFFECTIVE TEACHING

Judgement should be based on the extent to which teachers:

1. have a secure knowledge and understanding of subjects or areas they teach;

2. set high expectations so as to challenge pupils and deepen their knowledge and understanding;

3. plan effectively;

4. employ methods and organisational strategies which match curricular objectives and the needs of all pupils;

5. manage pupils well and achieve high standards of discipline;

6. use time and resources effectively;

7. assess pupils' work thoroughly and constructively, and use assessments to inform teaching;

8. use homework effectively to reinforce and/or extend what is learned in school.

Guidance on the Inspection of Secondary Schools *(The Stationery Office, 1995)*

What are your initial follow-up thoughts? For example:

> **?** Are there other factors which you feel are important in making an effective teacher? If so, where would you rank them, compared to the OFSTED list?

> **?** Are there any factors which are more important in contributing to the learning of boys and girls? If so, which are they? Why have you identified them?

Activity 2.2

Ask at least five colleagues in your school to identify the characteristics of an effective teacher. Ask them if there are any particular characteristics, which seem to be particularly successful in raising boys' achievement. **Do not show them the OFSTED list** – although you could do subsequently to compare thoughts and to encourage comments.

> **?** What are the similarities between the characteristics mentioned by your colleagues and those of OFSTED?

> **?** What are the differences?

> **?** Is there any commonality about the similarities and the differences? Can this be linked to anything specific – work-related issues, teaching styles, organisational factors, pupil–teacher relationships, discipline?

Activity 2.3

Ask a number of pupils, preferably a whole class, to list the characteristics of effective teachers and ineffective teachers. Ask them to rank them, as they result in successful or unsuccessful learning. Again, do not show them the OFSTED list.

Now consider the following:

> **?** Are there similarities between the characteristics mentioned, by the pupils, the teachers and OFSTED? Are there differences?
>
> **?** Is there any commonality about the similarities and the differences? Can this be linked to anything specific?
>
> **?** Is there any significance in the responses of underachieving pupils? Do they seem to highlight particular characteristics?
>
> **?** (In mixed-sex schools) Are there differences between the responses of the boys and the girls? If so, is it possible to put these differences into rough categories?
>
> **?** (In all-boys' schools) Are there clearly defined groups of boys according to responses?

Overall, have the responses of other colleagues and pupils surprised you in any way? The OFSTED list seems to stress the technical repertoire and skills of teachers, with an emphasis on the management of pupils' learning. Do your teachers and pupils agree with this?

Recent research suggests that pupils are more influenced by the human relationships aspects of teaching, and, for boys, this seems to be particularly marked (see chart below). Do your findings support or challenge this point of view?

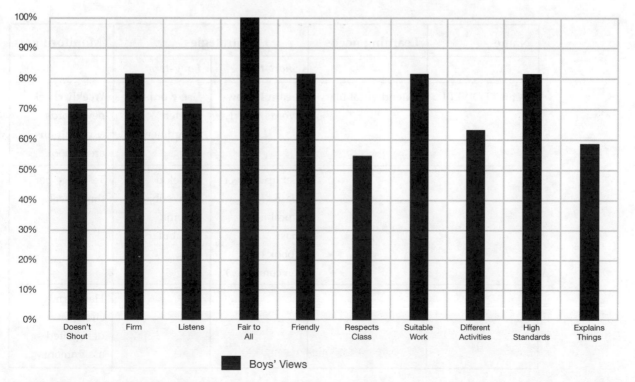

What Makes an Effective Teacher?: Boys' Views

Activity 3   Talking with Boys

Advanced Organiser

- ☞ **Link learning needs of some of your boys to learning strategies.**

- ☞ **Design monitoring activities to check on the success of the strategies.**

- ☞ **Reflect on the evidence base which could identify needs and strategies.**

- ☞ **Ask your group of boys to identify areas of need and support strategies.**

- ☞ **Compare, with the boys, your and their thoughts on ways forward.**

- ☞ **Agree with the boys short-term and long-term strategies to improve their learning.**

- ☞ **Monitor, review and move on together.**

Activity 3.1

Select five boys from your class or from one of your classes from across the ability range. Using a grid (see example below), make a list of strategies to raise their achievement. The strategies should include *short-term* and *long-term* plans to meet the individual boys' learning needs and the ways in which you will monitor the progress of these strategies.

Name	Learning needs	Strategies		Monitoring
		Short-term	*Long-term*	
Dennis POWELL	Extend vocabulary	Learn 10 new words weekly	Use words in written assignments	Weekly check; new words & definitions are in book
		Set up subject-based vocabulary base (book or on computer)	Develop area/subject specific vocabulary lists	Test once per three weeks
				Half-termly check on designated assignments

This process constructs an Individual Learning Plan for each boy. When you have produced a plan for all five boys, ask yourself:

? On what basis did you identify the learning need(s) of each boy? How was it evident in the work of each boy?

? Is/are the learning need(s) 'new' or 'ongoing'? If ongoing, what strategies have been attempted to address it/them? Has there already been any form of target setting or action planning?

? Have you talked to other colleagues about any of the boys?

? Are there any assessments or records which throw light on the needs and/or possible solutions?

? Has anyone else (parents, outside agencies, etc.) been involved in discussions about the boys' learning needs?

? Are there records of discussions with any of the boys about their learning?

? Have you discussed the boys' learning need(s) with them individually?

Gathering the opinions and insights from other people connected with the pupils will extend your understanding on how best to meet their needs.

Activity 3.2

Before putting the plan into action it is important to allow the boys themselves to consider, and then discuss with you, their perceptions of both their learning need(s) and the strategies which might help them to address those needs.

Stimulus Quotation 2

".... their [the pupils'] views deserve to be taken into account because they know, better than anyone, which teaching styles are successful, which techniques of learning bring the best out of them ....."

The Inner World of the School, *Cullingford, C. (Cassell, 1991)*

Ask the boys to complete the questionnaire on page 18.

Pupil Progress – Self Assessment

(A) Which subjects/areas of work do you need to improve in?

1..

2..

3..

4..

(B) What is stopping you from making progress in each subject/area of work? For example:

- spelling
- punctuation
- problems with reading
- writing in paragraphs
- remembering words

- understanding instructions
- noise in the class
- knowing what you have to do in lessons
- working quickly enough
- getting work finished on time

- unfair treatment by teachers
- the homework is too difficult
- not discussing the work enough
- remembering work you have done before.

There may be other things you can think of. Write your thoughts below.

Subject/Area of Work	Problems
1	
2	
3	
4	
Any others	

(C) What would help you to improve in each subject/area of work ?

Think of things that you can do to help yourself and things other people can do to help you.

Subject/Area of Work	Things you can do yourself	Things others can do to help (Say who they are – friends, teachers, parents, other pupils, etc.)
1		
2		
3		
4		

Do the same for the other subjects.

(D) What do you think you can improve on in each subject/area of work?

Subject/Area of Work	Improvement	
	In one week	In six weeks
1		
2		
3		
4		

Do the same for the other subjects.

Activity 3.3

Now compare your thoughts about each boy from activity 3.1 with what the boys have said. For each boy decide to what extent his perceptions agree with yours. Do the boys' responses make sense? Having seen their responses, do other strategies occur to you which you could add to their Independent Learning Plans?

Activity 3.4

'Conference' with each boy for five minutes. Discuss your thoughts and targets together. The aim is to come up with a joint action plan for each boy as a result of this. The action plan should include:

✓ A definition of the learning need(s).

✓ The short-term strategies needed to start addressing each learning need.

✓ The long-term strategies needed to address each learning need.

✓ The monitoring devices which will check on the success of the strategies. Include the agreed targets, the means for checking on progress, the timing of the monitoring, the personnel involved, any change to the targets, and the recording of any intervention/decisions.

✓ Dissemination of information to other people (to be agreed on) at stages to be agreed by you and each boy.

✓ Date for evaluation of progress.

Activity 4   Strategies Linked to Planned Activities

Advanced Organiser

☞ *Consider the importance of avoiding too much reflection and overplanning.*

☞ *Think of strategies for behaviour in class and around the school.*

☞ *Combine long-term strategies with planned 'quick' activities.*

☞ *Involve boys in designing and developing activities.*

Although it is important to think carefully about what you need to do to raise the achievement of boys, there is a danger that too much time spent thinking will cause inactivity and frustration. There is also a risk that overplanning the changes will lead to the completion of the plan becoming more important than developing as you go along. Given the extra dimension, shown in the last activity, of sharing thoughts and working on strategies with the boys themselves, it is all the more important to avoid assuming that you alone can come up with all the answers to individual boys' problems and needs.

So it is a good idea to develop your work with boys in two distinct but complementary ways. The first is to plan long-term, with a well-considered overall strategy, which can work systematically through the school over a long period of time. Some elements of this approach have been mentioned in the previous activity. The advantages of this approach are in the thoroughness and the depth of the changes which embed themselves in the ethos and the structures of the school.

The second way is to think of quick, relatively easy activities which make a noticeable impact on both the way boys see themselves and how they are seen by others. Although it is possible to argue that this 'fixing something quickly' approach is superficial, evidence shows that activity can galvanise people's thoughts and emotions, and help accelerate and give relevant shape to a strategy of long-term planning.

This activity comes in two parts – in your classroom and around the school. The classroom activity focuses your thoughts on the learning and behaviour of some of the boys you teach. The activity linked to the environment of the school asks you to consider what can be done to improve the status of boys around the school by involving them in raising the visible profile of a wide selection of boys.

Activity 4.1   Learning in the Classroom

Take your own or another class and try to think of one learning goal which each boy needs to achieve over the next academic year. Note down how you are going to evaluate the success of this learning goal. Then try to think of a 'fix it quickly' activity, linked to the longer-term strategy, which will enable each boy to see quickly signs of success that will please and motivate him.

Example

Boy	Learning Goal	Long-term Strategy	'Fix it quickly' Strategy
Paul	Improve quality of book reviews	To build up by stages the substance and structure of written book reviews. To be evaluated by the degree of independence shown in termly assessments linked to different reading stimuli. Stages of programme to be explained at outset and discussed throughout as progress is monitored.	Write book review to a format and structure provided on a worksheet. Display to high standard in classroom. Teacher to write home about success of outcome(s)

Activity 4.2   Behaviour in the Classroom

Do exactly the same activity, but replace learning with behaviour. Do not just choose boys who are poorly behaved. All boys should be considered to bring about positive behaviour for learning. This means not just thinking of strategies to modify bad behaviour, but also strategies which can develop confidence in the unconfident, assertiveness in the timid, collaboration in the isolated and independence in the over-reliant.

Activity 4.3 Around the School

The public face of the school, through the selectivity of displays, brochures and pamphlets, and the use of pupils in positions of public responsibility, gives out clear messages about the value that the school places on its pupils.

The absence of certain boys from the public face, either as learners or role models, can lead to quick re-enforcement of stereotypical attitudes. This part of the activity is designed to make you think about how you can use all boys (not necessarily all at the same time!) around the school as successful representatives of the school. This should include both examples of good work and participation in school events.

Using all the boys as quickly as possible in this public display of them as learners and role models is one of the best examples of how to combine a 'fixing something quickly' approach with a long-term strategy. Fixing something quickly provides immediate and tangible evidence of how pupils' work and broad contributions to the life of the school are valued. It is a clear example of how activity can be used to generate purpose and improvement in the ethos of a school without too much soul searching or deep management-type thinking. It is the activity itself which creates the deeper reflection and the conditions for more strategic planning about the management of learning. Activities have an essentially evolutionary quality to them, linking the small-scale to the broader strategy, and refining the strategy itself by its successes and failures.

Stimulus Quotation 3

"The objective of evolutionary planning is to capitalise on the 'low-risk' quality of smaller-scale innovation ... to increase certainty ...This in turn increases the motivation and the possibility of concerted more 'tightly coupled' action across the school."

Improving the Urban High School, *Louis K S and Miles M (Cassell, 1990)*

Displaying Work

Keep a checklist of the boys in a class. Ensure that every one of the boys contributes something to a display in a public area of the school. Clearly you will have to negotiate which area you can use. This in itself can often be a revealing and challenging issue! You will also have to decide which aspect of learning you intend to put on display, choosing something that lends itself to mass participation, with a wide variety of inputs. Bear in mind that contributions need not be restricted to having work on the display. The mounting, lettering and layout of the display are all important elements too.

A grid is a useful starting point. The example on page 22 is an illustrative one from a secondary school, but is easily adaptable to any phase – indeed many primary school teachers use this in their classrooms already.

Example

Focus of display	Elements required	Involvement of boys
Nazi election posters from 1930 election	A variety of posters (A3 size preferably) showing different aspects of Nazi election platform. Possible copying of original artwork & boys' own designs	10 boys at least
	Pictures/photographs in montage of Nazi election tactics – mixture of violent intimidation & use of mass media techniques	3 – 5 boys
	Examples of speeches, slogans, broadcasts used by Nazis (possible use of video/taped elements to display here)	3 – 5 boys
	Word-processed explanation of context of display, showing overt distaste for nature of the Nazis. Clear exposition of the sanitised version of the campaign compared with Nazi thoughts as indicated in *Mein Kampf*	3 – 5 boys
	Headings & captions	2 – 3 boys
	Layout & mounting	2 – 3 boys

Participating in School Events

As with the display about boys' learning, it is important that all of the boys should be encouraged to be representatives of the school at events and functions in which the public face of the school is high profile. Make a list of all the major events in the school year, before allocating boys to them equitably. Clearly the boys will need support and training before they can be 'let loose' on the public, but much of this can be done using the boys' own skills, experiences and sensibilities. Indeed, the boys will often come up with ideas that perhaps you had not even thought of !

Example

Events	No. of boys required	Names of boys
Parents' Evenings		
School Performances		
School Trips		
Reception Duties		
Open Days		
Sports Events		
Showing visitors round		
Playtime Duties		
Pupil Mentors (older ones mentoring younger ones)		
Assemblies		
Pupil Monitors (registers etc.)		

Involving the Boys in the Planning of Activities

One of the findings of school effectiveness questionnaires is that many teachers do not consider it important for pupils to be involved in school development planning. This would appear to preclude them from activities like the ones mentioned above. And yet, it seems hard to believe that pupils would not have some useful insights about what might help them to improve their learning, to develop positive behaviours, to contribute to work displays and the broader life of the school.

Involve pupils in all aspects of the above activities. Ask them all, individually (or a small, selected sample of them) to set themselves a short-term and long-term learning goal and behaviour goal, focused on the classroom. This should include suggested strategies for achieving the goals and ways of monitoring progress. Then ask them as a group to decide on suitable activities around the school, in terms of public displays and participation in school life, which they feel would show their talents and capabilities to best advantage.

Do their suggestions tally with yours?

Are the suggestions useful in complementing yours?

Are there common themes or are the suggestions and strategies unique to each boy?

Are their perceived needs only manageable by setting individual targets?

Then, AND ONLY THEN, consider implementing fully the 'fixing it quickly' and long-term strategies.

Activity 5   Drawing On Good Practice

Advanced Organiser

☞ **Identify a successful strategy you have used with a boy or groups of boys.**

☞ **Share successful strategies with a colleague.**

☞ **Design an action research initiative with a colleague(s).**

☞ **Contact a local school looking for successful strategies with boys.**

In this activity you are asked to draw on the successful experience that you and other colleagues have had in working with boys. Your experience with all boys may not have been successful, but it is likely that you will have been successful with at least one boy! And that is your starting point. He could be an achieving boy with whom you have developed successful strategies or an underachieving boy with whom who you have worked effectively. It does not matter: it is the fact that you have succeeded that is the important factor.

Start by noting down a successful strategy which you have used with an individual boy, a group of boys or various groups of boys.

Then think what the problem was. How did it relate to the boy(s)' learning needs? What evidence did you have for this ?

What was the strategy/strategies you chose to use? How did you arrive at this/these?

Discuss your strategy with a colleague and ask her/him to share a similar success story with you.

Are there common strands? Are there different strands which might relate to both of you in your different contexts?

It may be worth arranging to watch one another at work in the classroom with some of the boys. This might be illuminating, not just in the obvious way of seeing a strategy you might be able to use, but also in allowing you both to watch boys at work as an observer. Then you can discuss what you observed and develop a highly-prized relationship as 'critical friends'.

Have you both had other areas of success with boys? Is there a strategy you can 'swap' and try out with one or some of the boys you both teach? This could be the same boy(s) or different ones, who present similar sorts of challenges. Describe to each other how you are going to set about the 'action research' and arrange a formal time and date to review progress.

When this is done and you have decided what worked and what didn't, invite one other colleague each to attempt the same exercise. Broaden out in this way, taking more and more staff – and more and more boys – on board.

It is worth considering from the outset what criteria you have been using to measure success. Is it just 'academic' success, as measured in tests, assessments, reading scores, examinations. etc.? Or are there more qualitative measures you and your colleagues have come up with?

It is also worth thinking about what other local schools do with their boys. Do you know some that are successful? Making contact with a colleague at a school can be highly productive. Try to do this and go through a similar process as outlined above.

Activity 6   Resourcing the Raising of Boys' Achievement

Advanced Organiser

- ☞ *Invest resources carefully and in stages.*

- ☞ *Consider the time and effort that have gone into your work so far.*

- ☞ *Start small and manageable; build steadily on successes.*

- ☞ *Think about planning resource implications into any initiative.*

Throwing resources at a school-based initiative will not necessarily lead to successful outcomes. You will easily be able to point to examples in your own school and in other schools of failed initiatives, which have been either a complete waste of time and money or in which funding was invested at the wrong time, often too early and well before the initiative had been properly thought through.

But, is it possible in your school to introduce such a major initiative as raising boys' achievement without some extra resourcing? Consider how much time and effort you might need to do Activities 1–5 thoroughly as a group exercise in your school. What would you have to dispense with in your normal daily routines or developmental work just to start on your undertaking with boys, if you do not put in some extra resources?

Don't worry if there is not a huge amount of resources available. You might want to start small anyway. This is probably a better and safer bet than going for a grand scheme, as the latter often leads to overstretching, disappointment and frustration. It may be more realistic to consider a manageable project, which targets particular year groups or identified groups of underachieving boys. This helps to keep the resource issue in its perspective – and under control. So when starting on this activity, try to keep a good balance between the resources you might need to get things underway and the absolute necessity to be cost effective with the school's money. After all, there are other demands on both time and money.

Stimulus Quotation 4

"To argue that large sums of money are vital to change is to provide an excuse for inaction. While resourcing is important, the Halton [Canada] experience raises questions about the need for large sums of money to effect significant change."

Changing Our Schools, *Stoll L and Fink D (Open University, 1996)*

Using the grid below draw up an initiative for your school to raise boys' achievement, bearing in mind that you need to aim for a sustainable long-term strategy, whilst thinking about a 'quick fix' or two which you might be able to implement successfully.

Strategy	Activity	Resources		
		Human	Time	Financial
(1) Establishing causes of underachievement				
(2) Understanding how teaching meets the learning needs of boys				
(3) Talking with boys about strategies to meet learning needs				
(4) Planned activity to raise the achievement of boys				
(5) Drawing on good practice within and outside own school				

Reflections on Section One

The activities in this first section will probably have shown you how complex the issues of boys' achievement are, even at a very local level – your school. Thoughts on the causes of the underachievement of boys are varied and interesting (see page 27), as are the strategies that people suggest to address underachievement.

Causes of Boys' Underachievement

Widely-held perceptions

1. Girls are cleverer than boys.
2. Adolescence affects boys more than girls.
3. Girls get more attention than boys.
4. Girls are better at coursework than boys.
5. Young boys have very few 'good' male role models at home and in school.
6. Changes in employment patterns have affected girls more than boys.
7. Boys pay less attention to homework than girls.
8. The equal opportunities initiatives of the 1980s have worked against boys.
9. Boys do not read as widely as girls. They fall behind at primary school and never close the gap.
10. Boys are more independent than girls, and are more 'anti-authority'.

Although it is possible to look at the 'average' boy, as the media seem to be doing at present, you will have noticed how unique boys are, exactly as girls are. Nonetheless, there may be common strands which are useful in general terms, but your strategies will depend very much on the needs of the boys in your school and the particular strategies that the school can adopt to support them. What your boys say will help you to identify closely these needs and the teaching and learning strategies to work on them. Moreover, involving the boys will give an extra element of legitimacy to your efforts.

Before moving on, consider the do's and don'ts set out below. Refer back to them as you continue your work to raise boys' achievement.

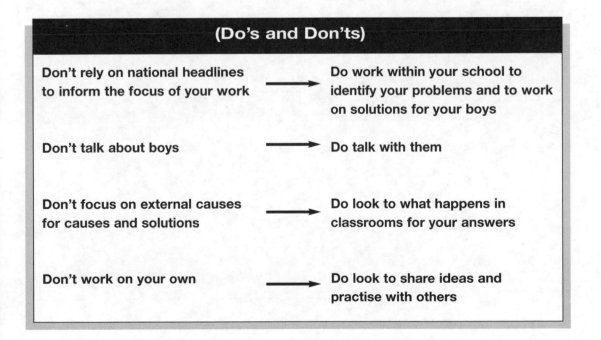

(Do's and Don'ts)

Don't rely on national headlines to inform the focus of your work	Do work within your school to identify your problems and to work on solutions for your boys
Don't talk about boys	Do talk with them
Don't focus on external causes for causes and solutions	Do look to what happens in classrooms for your answers
Don't work on your own	Do look to share ideas and practise with others

In this part of the book you are invited to compare the boys in your school with the widely held views of many experts, academics and the media about the causes of and solutions to the underachievement of boys. In the previous section you identified some of the important issues related to working with boys, and you have looked in some detail at the possible causes of boys' underachievement in your own school.

Part Two goes deeper into the subject and helps you build up a body of baseline information, on which you can base meaningful and lasting strategies with your underachieving boys. On the way you may challenge or support the widespread perceived wisdom about boys' underachievement. You will probably develop some strategies all of your own. You may make mistakes as well! But it is important that you take these risks and test your theories, as long as those theories are based firmly on hard evidence which you have gathered from your boys – about why some of them underachieve and what can be done together to improve achievement.

Part Two also asks you to test your experiences against the commonly held views that boys' underachievement is caused by:

> - *Their attitudes to school.*
>
> - *Socio-economic factors, including male peer group pressure and single-parent families.*
>
> - *Unalterable biological factors.*
>
> - *The influence of school.*
>
> - *Equal opportunities issues.*
>
> - *Central government policy initiatives.*

They can be solved by:

> - *Encouraging boys to be as positive as girls about school.*
>
> - *Challenging the 'macho' anti-school culture of many boys.*
>
> - *Developing analytical skills in boys.*
>
> - *Having more successful male role models in schools, especially at primary school level.*
>
> - *Helping boys to be more flexible and open in their attitudes to employment pathways.*
>
> - *Less girl-friendly coursework and continuous assessment in public examinations.*

Each section looks briefly at the commonly held causes for boys' underachievement, and a range of corresponding solutions. It might be tempting to gloss over the causes and move straight to practical solutions, but it would be unwise to do so. It would be possible to see the causes as mere problems, which are then dwelled upon and agonised over, thus avoiding getting on with the strategies, which will change things. But any 'suggested' solutions are so inextricably linked to the causes that it is vital to test the validity of the causes before considering them. Your findings about the causes of your boys' underachievement may be similar to the 'public' view of boys, but they may also seem to contradict one, some, or all of the perceived wisdom about boys'. underachievement.

It is more likely that your solutions will throw up a mixture of agreements and contradictions. This is hardly surprising. Your situation is unique, and the findings will be unique to your school. It is your findings that count, provided they are based on serious reflection about and with your boys. Without these findings, you will not be able to develop focused strategies.

The solutions include a variety of strategies to raise the standards of achievement of boys. Some of these will be challenged, some will be recommended and others will be left 'unproved'. Each will be considered for their practical effectiveness in improving the learning of all boys. Again you will be invited to consider the strategies which might be taken wholesale, in part, or in combination to suit your school's needs.

At the end of each section there will be a case study, which illustrates one approach to raising boys' achievement linked to the particular discussion points in that section.

Section Two

Boys' Attitudes to School

Advanced Organiser

☞ *Consider if boys are less committed to school work than girls, and whether they care less about education.*

☞ *Use questionnaires which can identify attitudinal issues.*

☞ *Use in-depth interviews with boys to add more depth and detail to questionnaire information.*

☞ *Consider the importance of looking into effective learning preferences and strategies.*

1   Cause

There is a considerable amount of research evidence to support anecdotal suggestions that the attitudes of boys towards education in general and school in particular explain partly their recent poor examination achievement in comparison with girls.

Stimulus Quotation 5

"Indeed most [boys] are concerned only with 'passing', not with 'excelling' or even 'doing well'. The language of 'passing' a test, or 'passing' a course dominates ... discourse."

Working Class Without Work, *Weis, L (Routledge, 1990)*

This North American study in a secondary school is supported by the massive ongoing survey being carried out by the Centre for Successful Schools at Keele University. This survey of nearly 30,000 pupils shows that boys' attitudes to school differ significantly from girls. By four per cent to be precise – interestingly enough, roughly the same percentage difference as in GCSE and 'A' level examination results !

Pupil Commitment to Learning by Year and Sex

	KEY STAGE 3 Years 7 – 9		KEY STAGE 4 Years 10 – 11		VIth Form		Gender		Total
	M	F	M	F	M	F	**M**	**F**	
School Totals for 1995	8822	8564	5289	5339	338	441	14649	14496	29145
% showing commitment	65.5	69.4	60.0	65.4	63.4	68.8	63.3	67.9	65.6

Young People and their Attitudes to School, Centre for Successful Schools, (Keele Univ., 1994)

One of the things you may wish to do in your school is to start by employing the services of a Higher Education Institute, like Keele University, or Homerton College, Cambridge, and the Institute of Education, London, which have developed schemes to sample pupils' views and feed back the information to you. This can be done for the whole school, or for particular ages or groupings.

There is also a questionnaire package, *Ethos Indicators in Schools*, which was developed jointly by the Scottish Office Education Department (SOED) and a research team led by Professor John MacBeath. This provides very useful information for schools on what pupils say about various aspects of their learning and life in school. You can devise your own, of course!

You could try the following pupils' questionnaire immediately with your boys and girls to compare their attitudes. If your school is an all-boys school, try to encourage a neighbouring all-girls school to join you, as an interesting comparative case study. Failing this, there is no real problem, as it is not the comparison alone that is all important. Rather it is what underlies the results and what this might be telling you about all the boys, some boys, a few of the boys, specific ability groupings, particular teaching classes, age groups or ethnic groups. The key for you is where the positive attitudes seem to be and where the less positive are.

Pupil Attitudes Questionnaire				
(A) The School in General	All the time	Most of the time	Sometimes	Never
1. I enjoy being at school				
2. School work is interesting				
3. Teachers are nice to everyone				
4. I think this is a good school				
5. Some children are naughty				
6. I like to help others in the classroom				
7. I get bullied by other pupils				
8. I go to after school activities				
9. I like most of the pupils in the class				
10. I feel unsafe in the playground				
(B) Learning and Teaching	Yes		No	Don't know
11. I am good at school work				
12. My teacher(s) tell me off				
13. I mess around in class				
14. I am bored in lessons				
15. If I get school work to do at home I do it as well as I can				
16. Boys don't behave as well as girls in school				
17. Girls work harder than boys				
18. Boys don't bother as much about school work as girls				
19. Boys are given more attention in class than girls				
20. Girls care more about learning than boys				

Raising Boys' Achievement

These questions are adapted largely from the pupil questionnaires in *Ethos Indicators in Schools* (SOED) and *Differential Achievement of Girls and Boys at GCSE* (Homerton College, Cambridge).

When your pupils have completed this, you can analyse the information and decide what you want to do with it. The danger is that you might be 'satisfied' with the results rather than acting upon them, especially as questionnaires can be limited in the information they provide. Backing up the results with a series of interviews of the boys can be illuminating. If you have time try to interview half the sample, but if not, at least five.

By structuring the interview around the issue of what boys feel about learning you may find that the results show some variations from the questionnaire figures. Certainly you will have more depth, and you may have some clues to where the boys' attitudes are coming from. This can help you see how these might be used to channel individual boys' attitudes into learning approaches that work. In aggregate, you might still feel that boys' attitudes are different from girls, but you should see now that individual boys have many different attitudes from one another.

Hopefully you will discover that boys do care about their education as much as girls. As a group they may show this caring in a less 'acceptable', more challenging way than many girls, but as individuals they care just as much. As teachers we have to accept and work with the individual differences of all pupils, not resent those who seem not to fit our desired image of the willing and motivated learner.

Stimulus Quotation 6

"The difference between [gender] differences is smaller than the difference within groups."

Improving Boys' Performance, *Hannan G (Inset Materials, 1996)*

---

2   Solution

One suggestions to improve boys' achievement is to make them more like girls in their attitudes to school work. But this ignores two key interrelated factors linked to Hannan's comment above.

First, not all girls achieve particularly well, with significant differences from school to school, and from subject to subject within these schools. Second, some boys achieve very well indeed, but also with significant differences from school to school, and from subject to subject within these schools. It might be more profitable from an individual school's point of view to explore what makes some pupils successful learners rather than trying to make boys learn like girls, and to assume that all girls will be successful because, well, all girls do well, don't they!

Take five boys in your class who are doing well in terms of attitude and achievement to school. Try to list attitudinal characteristics which seem to make them successful learners. Is it possible to isolate those attitudinal factors which make these particular boys successful, other than saying that they are well motivated, interested, positive or enthusiastic about learning? For instance, do these boys all learn in the same way? Try to work out if each one is :

- a *pragmatist* who likes to get on with things; is impatient with reflective discussion; takes the first opportunity to see if things work in practice; searches out new ideas to apply

- a *theorist* who likes to think problems through in stages; likes to analyse things; is keen on basic principles, theories and thinking; links facts to theory

- a *reflector* who likes to stand back and observe; values the collection and analysis of information; listens to others and likes to be part of a broad picture

- an *activist* who likes to get involved in any new learning experience; enjoys the present; is open-minded and likes brainstorming; gets involved with others.

Adapted from **The Manual of Learning Styles**, *Honey P and Mumford A, (Maidenhead, 1986)*

Thinking about the learning attitudes of individuals and developing strategies for boys is potentially more interesting and beneficial to your teaching than questioning individual attitudes based on generalisations about them out of your context.

If you have a mixed class, try the same exercise with five successful girls. Are there significant differences from the boys which are more marked than any significant similarities? Do they all, the boys and girls, exhibit similar 'attitudes', but a wide range of learning approaches? If they do, then it is highly likely that it is success at the 'learning game' which has led to positive attitudes to school rather than the other way round. In many walks of life and activities, people are motivated by things they have learned to do to the best of their ability, including learning how to learn successfully. There are very few people who can retain a positive attitude in the face of constant and persistent failure!

The real test of the work in this section is to take your boys and see if you can honestly attribute gender as the sole cause of successful or unsuccessful attitudes to work. Are these attitudes solely confined to gender, or can you identify other factors which are just as, or even more, significant? Is the solution really for boys to be more like girls, or is that to deny the possibility that deeper thinking about learning for all pupils might bring about better standards of achievement rather than focusing on gender attitudes?

The fact that there are boys in your school who are 'switched on' despite their gender suggests that the 'switched off' attitude of other boys is not solely attributable to gender.

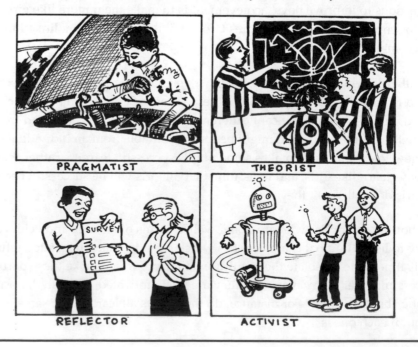

Case Study One

Abbey Wood School, South-East London

This case study charts the work done in a mixed secondary school by a small Art department, which raised the achievement of pupils by focusing on the quality of the teaching and learning. That it 'solved' the underachievement of boys came as a by-product of an overall drive to raise standards, rather than by focusing on them specifically. The case study has been adapted from thoughts written down by Richard Cowley, Head of Art.

The GCSE examination results in Art have risen for both boys and girls, from 10 per cent achieving grades A-C in 1992 to 74 per cent gaining grade A*-C in 1996. This raising of achievement and its acceleration reflects the ability of the departmental staff to be adaptable and confident enough to change their teaching styles, through the acceptance of new ideas and strategies and the willingness to share their expertise with others.

What we established first on coming together as a staff was that we needed a common set of principles and practices, a comprehensive set of policies that addressed every facet of the teaching and learning experience. We wrote a departmental handbook and that has been re-visited twice to date, and a further review is planned this year. Most of the documentation is 'live' and in use in our planning, assessment and recording procedures. It is not a handbook that, once written, is left on the shelf to gather dust. Nor is it carved in stone and sacrosanct. At the very start of our partnership we produced a department development plan and action plan. We are not slaves to the timetable of events we propose, but we do check and chase one another to implement strategies and initiatives, and we update both plans every year.

Through the vehicle of an annual common theme for all students, we are able to set a tradition in the displays of work, which enables each student to see the sequence and progression of work from Years 7 to 11. The display changes in character and imagery each year, reflecting the differences between students as individuals and reinforcing the range of skills and knowledge.

Our policies include us working together to evaluate each other's teaching rooms, displays and resource management. We review both common and individual projects, and invite help and advice from one another on lesson planning, the management of lessons, teaching strategies and through visiting each other's lessons.

With the students we aim to create a climate of confidence. To achieve this we use the theme to engage, motivate and inspire the student. The purpose is to challenge and confront them with their own experiences, values, prejudice and ignorance in the light of current issues which relate to the social, cultural, spiritual and economic. This involves the student fully in the process of developing a personal response and imagery within a structured framework.

We explore the theme using a variety of starting points, choosing one or more according to the development point in the course structure. These range from brainstorming techniques, listing for-and-against arguments, games and quizzes, media information and investigation, recording and analysis of actual and created environments – still life, working outdoors/indoors.

The process is one of information gathering, the development of visual literacy and language, the use of a wide range of perceptual processes, critical and contextual studies, cross-curricular studies, and media and support methods, e.g. photocopies, photographs, tracing, overhead projection as well as first-hand observation.

The learning process is seen as a continuum, and we aim to avoid demotivating the student through destructive criticism. We work hard at helping the students cope with setbacks and difficulties, and we encourage them to see these for what they are – challenges and opportunities to learn.

Our specific practices contain many of the practices common to all Art departments. How we 'mix and match' these is important in developing the confidence of students, exciting their interest and maintaining motivation.

Contrast and *change* are perhaps the keys for us when planning activities. Some of the strategies we use are: change in a drawing programme from drawing with a pencil to scene painters' charcoal or brush or to monoprint or collage; from small pieces of paper (postage stamp size) to twice A1; working individually, as pairs, groups or whole class; individual display of work to composite whole class display (on the school hall wall – 10 metres x 7 metres). Painting, printing and three-dimensional work programmes are managed in the same way, and processes are combined often. We tend to work large, twice A1 size, to encourage using the full body (standing, arm and wrist movement), with students working on the wall or floor, as well as tables. Small finger movement work can be restrictive and difficult for young people, and this process helps them to understand their physical and artistic development.

We were able to put in place much of the above quickly and we have spent time since refining our practices and becoming more aware of the fact that we operate best as a team. Given the expectations and workload in education today, I believe it would be impossible to have a life outside teaching if we were not sharing the work between us.

Because we operated as a team and believed that all our students could raise their levels of achievement, we initially targeted Years 10 and 11 in 1992 for extra lessons after school. Our work addressed and focused on key elements missing from their education. We cajoled, pursued them, and picked them off one by one. We wanted to get an instant tradition of good work. Many of the students wanted to do good work. It was really that simple, combined with the thematic stimulus and systematic development of skills. It was hard work, requiring commitment from staff and students.

For Years 8 and 9 we operated a recovery scheme within the programmes of work, and, as they progressed into Years 10 and 11, they automatically did extra work after school. It is now part of the expectation and tradition.

Section Three

Boys and Peer Group Pressure

Advanced Organiser

☞ **Gender identity is key to making boys anti-school.**

☞ **Boys' views about school depend on the setting in which they talk.**

☞ **Schools need to offer a less 'aggressive' image of what it means to be a successful boy.**

☞ **'Achieving' boys can give clues about how to cope with peer pressure.**

1 Cause

For most boys it is more important to be 'one of the lads' than it is to work hard in school. A common view is that having a laugh or mucking about is what boys do well, and school work does not come naturally to them. Whether it is spending hours playing football or computer games, just hanging around with mates, drinking themselves silly and fighting, or taking drugs, that's what makes most boys tick. Or so the story goes!

But is this true for most boys? And, even if there is some truth in it, what are the influential factors that bring this about, and is there anything within them which might hint at possible solutions? More importantly, are these issues of such underlying significance and so deep-seated that they can prevent schools from raising some boys' achievement?

Let us consider the argument that most boys are 'anti-school' and under pressure to be so. It has been argued that gender identity is crucial for boys and girls from a very early age. It is well documented that boys' attitudes are clearly anti-school by the end of primary school, yet it is assumed commonly that Year 8 or Year 9 is the key turning point for boys. At this time, the argument goes, boys begin to assert their masculinity by increased resentment and defiance of the school as authority. School work becomes low priority, compared with the drive to socialise, play sport or monopolise play stations. Panic, or comparative panic, sets in only when public examinations are nearly upon them, or coursework deadlines are the following day. For some the panic never even sets in and they opt out of school altogether.

But recent research suggests that the key point is an earlier one at primary school. At this stage, early on in Key Stage 2, boys take on, as part of their gender development, a desire to be as 'unfemale' as possible. Between the ages of three and seven they are aware, like girls, of the concept of gender difference, but only at about eight does it become a defining, key issue for them. This can be seen, for example, in reading, where the development of a reading identity, based on what boys are enjoying reading, starts to clash with the development of their gender identity.

A study in Australian primary schools in the late 1980s showed that all children come to school knowing that they are girls or boys. They have a strong commitment to being members of their gender group and this includes a potential antagonism towards the other gender. In their struggle to be seen clearly as a boy, most boys begin to attempt to show that they are true boys, warriors in fact. But few reach warrior status and have to settle for next best.

Stimulus Quotation 7

"..... boys also have available to them a weaker definition of masculinity as 'not female' and this allows them to redress insecurities and ambivalences by ..... showing through their contempt for and harassment of girls, that they are definitely male ....."

from **Gender and Education** *Vol.7, No.1, Jordan E (Carfax, 1995)*

By secondary school the boys' notion of difference has developed into one of conscious superiority over girls, with 'being male', according them, a higher status than being a girl. Positive attitudes to, and success in, schooling are at odds with the development of masculinity. By this stage the pressure on boys to conform to the gender stereotype of not working at school is overwhelmingly strong for many of them. If they cannot be the main anti-school figures, by disruption, truancy or lack of work, at least they can belong to the second rank, and not work hard or appear to be enjoying school work. And so peer group pressure builds inexorably, based on the boys' development of the male identity, as a conscious attempt not to be female.

But does this fit the reality of what boys feel, or is it an adult interpretation of what we think happens, or what we want to think happens? The best way to find out is to ask the boys themselves what they think. And there are two distinct stages to this exercise – three if your school is a mixed one.

Stage One
Ask small groups of boys to describe what it means for a boy to learn in school. This can be done in various ways, and with different degrees and expectations of complexity, depending on the age of the boys.

For young boys, about age seven or under, a small group of five or six boys is ideal. The best approach is to use a structured group interview, with about ten questions, which are trying to tease out two issues. These are, first, whether the boys have common attitudes to their learning as a group, and, second, if they see themselves as having different attitudes to learning from girls.

Obviously, you will be trying to discover if these young boys already have a shared view about their gender as learners, if they see themselves as being less positive than girls about school work, and if they feel under any kind of gender pressure not to work hard. The boys may even volunteer explanations about why these things obtain! You may find it useful to record these interviews on to cassette, so that you can play back what the boys say rather than relying on frantically-taken notes. But beware, as it usually takes about five times longer than the interviews themselves to playback cassettes, transcribe and analyse them.

You can devise your own questions to suit the needs of your boys, but below are some suggestions.

(1)   What do you like doing most of all in class?

(2)   Why do you like doing this?

(3)   Do your friends like doing the same things as you in class? Who are they?

(4)   What do you not like learning in school at the moment? Why?

(5)   Do most of the boys in your class like doing the same things? Why do you think that is?

(6)   Do you ever work with girls in your class? Do they like the same sorts of things as you?

(7)   Do most girls and boys work as hard as each other? Which girls work harder? Which boys work harder?

(8)   Do boys and girls like school work as much as each other?

(9)   Do other boys stop you working? Does this happen often?

(10)   If another boy asks you to mess around in class, do you do it instead of your work? Why (not)?

For older boys, aged roughly between seven and 14, you could use the questions above to stimulate a structured group discussion or you could simply ask the groups to have a discussion about boys' attitudes to work. The eventual outcome of this would be a profile of boys' and girls' attitudes to work, trying to identify similarities and differences in the form of a chart, checklist or pictorial display. Additionally, there should be some attempt to tease out if boys feel under any kind of pressure not to work and why.

For boys aged 14 and over, there could be a group discussion/debate around the topic 'Boys can't be seen to work as hard as girls at school'. In this it is worth encouraging some of the boys to try to step out of role, and to argue against the statement. By doing this in a formal situation, it is possible to give boys the 'authority' or 'licence' to put the case for the absence of peer group pressure.

For all of these approaches, determined in complexity by age, the key factor is to establish the boys' group view. Do they as a group believe that there is a gender difference in attitudes to school work, and do they also think there is such a thing as peer group pressure, which is very much anti-work? Moreover, if these exist where do they come from?

When you have finished the activity, make a list of your findings under the following headings:

	Boys' Attitudes to Work	Girls' Attitudes to Work	Peer Group Pressure
(1)			
(2)			
(3)			
(4)			
(5)			

Stage Two

After a week or so repeat the same exercise with the same group of boys, but on their own. For the younger boys, simply ask the same questions individually, record them and transcribe the tapes. For the older group, either ask them to write down their answers to the questions or to do a short piece of writing, 'Boys' and girls' attitudes to school work – what is the same and what is different? If there are differences, why do you think there are?' Then analyse the responses, using the same headings you had for the group exercise.

What you are likely to find is that there is an absence or weakening of the element connected to the notion of peer group pressure.

There is evidence that boys accept readily that there is such a thing as peer group pressure, and that they acknowledge this whether they are asked to comment about it in large groups, small groups or on their own. But there are two common contradictions shown by most boys individually to this generalised acknowledgement. Firstly, many boys say that they are not personally affected by peer group pressure, whilst admitting that it is quite a common feature in and out of schools. Secondly, many of them say also that peer group pressure does not work as a blanket factor. Rather it is partial in aspect, and is linked to which teacher sets them work, whether work is acceptable because it has a deadline/examination connection, or, in the case of homework, if you can get away with doing the bare minimum or nothing at all.

What seems to be crucial for many boys is to retain a balance in their lives. It is perfectly all right to work hard at school and be seen to be achieving, as long as you have a life outside school with other interests. What is unacceptable is to work hard and enjoy it when the teaching is unstimulating and the work uninspiring or unchallenging.

The Boys' Perspective

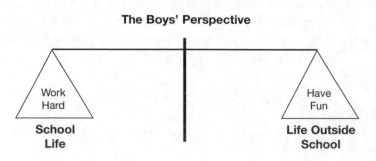

You may be able or confirm or refute your findings and my research by attempting the next step:

Stage Three
This involves asking small groups of girls the same questions as you asked the groups of boys in *Stage One*. You will have to change questions (5) and (6) round to ask girls if they ever work with boys, and you will also have to change questions (9) and (10), in order to ask these girls if they notice boys putting pressure on other boys not to work in school.

It might also be interesting to ask the girls one further question, namely, 'Do you think boys dislike girls who work hard?' If the girls say yes, follow this up by asking them 'What do they say or do to show this?'

What can often be illuminating when talking to girls about boys' attitudes, is their readiness to support many boys' views about their learning. Admittedly, they will often refer to boys having a more casual attitude to work, liking to have a laugh, messing about or trying to impress them and other boys. But they will also say that boys tend to get told off more by teachers for bad behaviour, disproportionately so given the levels of disruption by boys and girls. Many also believe that boys' learning is more affected by their relationship with their teachers and the quality of those teachers.

But despite the research evidence, there is still a strongly and widely-held view that peer group pressure is the most significant single factor in the underachievement of boys. And it is a highly persuasive argument, linked as it is to the development of gender identity, and the different reaction of the genders in a changing world. In this changing world, males are failing to cope with the loss of their traditional securities – the best jobs, the best examination results, and the dominant position within the family locally and within society at large. Their attitudes, successful in the past, are no longer so.

2 Solution
There is a widely-held view that if schools can 'crack' the anti-school attitude of many boys, then the strength of peer group pressure will weaken. There are two strands to the argument. The first argument is that encouraging boys to be less 'macho', indeed more 'girl-like', by conforming to school expectations about work levels and behaviour patterns, will foster a climate in which boys feel more positive about their work. This will lead to boys' willingness to do more than just enough to get by, and to be more receptive to a public celebration of working hard at school.

The second argument is that making school more attractive to boys will lead to fewer reasons for them to kick against an environment which they see as alien and unexciting. This will give school greater resonance for boys and create an atmosphere in which boys do not feel the need to be anti-girl, because girls no longer approach school in a distinctive way. Both these arguments have in common a desire to change patterns of boys' behaviour and, thus, make them like school more.

But will this work? Is it possible to stop boys wanting to be identified in terms of gender as successful fighters or warriors?

Stimulus Quotation 8

"(Most boys adopt) ... a definition of masculinity that has femininity as the subordinate term, the cycle whereby the resistance of the 'fighting' boys establishes an identification of their behaviour with the 'warrior' discourse and forces parents and teachers who want the boys to take advantage of the benefits the school provides ... to offer an alternative definition of masculinity as 'not female'. I have suggested that instead teachers and parents should concentrate on showing that resistance to the authority of the school is not the only way of living out the 'warrior' definition, that they should engage, and engage the children, with the complexities of the discourse and point out that to a considerable degree violence and destructiveness are the subordinate term in the definition of masculinity."

from **Gender and Education** *Vol.7, No.1, Jordan E (Carfax, 1995)*

Complex as the language may be, the message is clear. If schools can offer boys a masculinity which is not dependent on physical toughness, then boys can start to compete with girls and one another on those issues that will channel energies into the raising of achievement.

But is it really that simple? How, for instance, are you going to impact on the 'macho' nature of some of the boys? Will a direct challenge have an effect? Will it be possible to do this by stealth? Above all, is it possible or wise to apply this principle to all boys in a blanket way?

Try it! Take a group of boys in (one of) your class(es), choosing three or so who are doing well and an equal number who are not doing well. If you have girls as well, then choose an equal number of them. Identify the characteristics which make the successful learners successful, and those characteristics of the less successful ones which are causing problems in learning. Do this for each of the pupils in turn, working hard to base your thoughts on hard evidence, not on intuition or gut feeling. For 'unsuccessful' pupils, simply change the headings.

Remember that the purpose of this activity is to discover if there is value in trying to change boys' attitudes to work either by changing their macho views or by changing the school's way of operating to accommodate boys. So it is important that you use observed or recorded information, rather than your perceptions of what you think might be causing success or the lack of it. Time-consuming though it might be, you might find it informative to talk to the boys themselves, either while you are doing the activity or shortly afterwards.

Pupil	Success Indicators	Reasons for Success
	Achievement	(1) Prior Attainment
		(2) Parental Support
		(3) Peer Group Support
	Commitment	(4) Response to Teaching
		(5) Willingness to Achieve Targets
		(6) Gender Issues
		(7) Other (specify below)

When you have finished working with all your pupils, list the success indicators, so that you can see what the 'defendable' evidence would be for any possible generalisations about success or lack of it. Then try to create a composite picture of the reasons for success and compare these with the reasons why some pupils are not being successful. If you have had a group of girls to work with, you can compare them as well, putting the boys and girls together, and then comparing them in terms of gender.

If your findings indicate that issues around gender are a common factor with unsuccessful boys, then there may be a case for arguing that peer group pressure affects potential for achievement. However, you are then left trying to find an explanation for what makes the achieving boys successful. How are they able to avoid the pressure of other boys? Do they avoid 'contact' with unsuccessful boys? Do they deflect them somehow?

If you have included girls, what makes them unsuccessful? It is possible that your findings show that the issues relate more to the development of a successful learning identity, caused by a number of factors. These include pupils' understanding and application of learning strategies, the use of the support for learning which adults can provide, and the learning context which the pupils come from, rather than the power of gender identity working alone.

Certainly you will have found that the explanation for boys' underachievement is complex. Gender may be a significant factor, but it is not the only one. Furthermore, a solution based on schools changing boys' gender identity or being more attractive to boys as a homogeneous group is likely to miss the mark. Such a solution does not acknowledge or respond to the full range of factors which inhibit the learning development of all pupils.

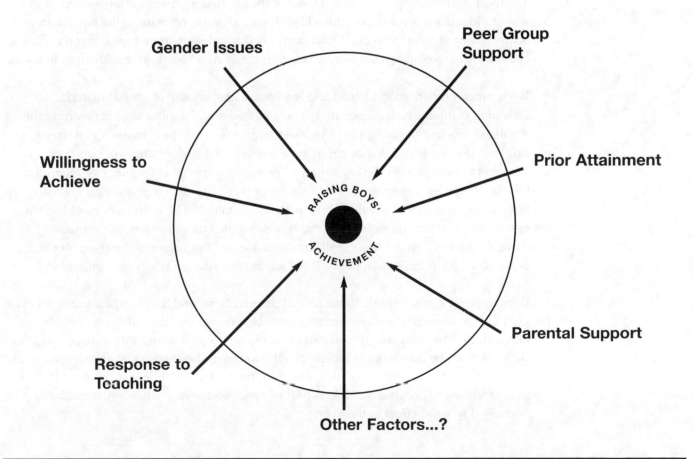

Case Study Two

Hitchin Boys' School, Hertfordshire

The following consists of extracts from an analysis of work with Year 10, 11 and 12 boys during 1995/1996, carried out and written by Head of English, Julia Dalton and considers strategies for teaching English to boys. Julia is currently Deputy Head of St. George's School, Harpenden.

Until I worked as Head of English in a boys' comprehensive school, I was convinced that gender issues, other than those intended to secure equal opportunities in the widest sense, were an invention of an age obsessed with making schools the repository for all the ills of society. The British have never been good at accepting children as an integral part of the human race, preferring to delegate responsibilities to nannies, social services or schools. It was with some reluctance, then, that I came to be involved with the current debate, now fuelled by a barrage of statistics concerning the achievement of boys in national examinations.

Following a particularly disturbing *Panorama* programme and several articles in the press, I thought – having several hundred boys between the ages of 11 and 18 as living evidence in the school – that I would ask them to examine themselves and the issues. Self-awareness is not a quality most of us work to develop, but the young tend to be more candid, and their logic is not confused by the bulging baggage of the guilt and angst carried by adults. From what they said and wrote I collected some surprising evidence about their perception of the ways boys work (in secret), think about school systems (only the people who teach them really matter) and respond to the media coverage of their perceived lack of motivation and achievement (very defensively).

The multiple complexities of contemporary society make generalisations odious, but I want to identify a few factors which I believe are directly relevant to the behaviour and achievement of boys in school. Only when I had spent some time evaluating these, could I begin to plan teaching strategies with these 'new' needs and challenges in mind.

Boys, much more than girls, read and look at a wider variety of textual material. Very little of it, comparatively, is fiction. We may have made the mistake of bemoaning the demise of reading amongst 12/13 year-old boys, when what we mean is that they give up reading story books. We ought to introduce a much wider variety of non-fiction stimulus resources from the beginning of Year 7. The specialist language of mountain bike or computer magazines is a rich source of work for language analysis, and can give boys an expertise in its use that you are unable to match. The technicalities of bicycle suspension systems are unlikely to provide dramatic entertainment, but explaining them, or the finer points of football commentaries, or the jargon of the computer buff, can give value to individual interests, which in turn adds to language competency.

Boys respond better, I think, to the formal presentation/oral/public speaking tasks than girls. It is so essential to success in any work beyond school, that all young people can talk confidently, and present views and ideas in an accessible and informative way; but such work in the classroom is especially vital to boys. They should be encouraged to use overhead projectors and visual aids, and told that formal interview is being replaced by the presentation. Because bravado is part of their defensive mechanism, it can be harnessed to good effect in this way.

The standards of quality in most forms of journalism are very high. Most columnists use English superbly well, and the use of metaphor or imagery can be as productively studied through the sports pages of *The Times* or *Daily Telegraph* as through poetry. Boys read things that English teachers of my vintage wouldn't ever come across – so let them teach you something. It is for this reason that I would offer Language and Literature at both GCSE and A level, because the creative, analytical and 'scientific' study of a variety of English for different purposes is much more important to boys than girls. In my A level group at my present school, dominated by girls, there is an overriding need on their part to be led through the text – I had forgotten how much it matters to girls to know what the teacher expects and to feel secure.

In teaching methods, or rather mechanisms for enhancing learning, there are important differences in the ways boys set about completing an essay or producing coursework. Long-term targets are just unrealistic, when there are always more interesting or less strenuous ways of passing the time. Essays in stages are better tactics with boys. The final write up, after drafting and preparation have been carefully monitored, is best done under 'controlled conditions', even if this is not exam work. An hour of supervised concentration in order to achieve a finished piece of work is worth weeks of frustration when homework and re-drafts are mislaid or forgotten.

There are few boys, either in a single-sex or mixed environment, who would wish to be seen as conscientious. To be acknowledged as clever is just bearable, but to show off about it, or use the good brain for school work in public is simply not cool. You must seem in control and amused at all times, but you are at liberty to be 'perfectly miserable in private'. Confrontations over work, or the lack of it, or behaviour, unless carefully planned, are seen as deliberate humiliation. Praise in private, punish in private. Treat each boy as an individual – they have the perception that girls are not 'lumped together' for criticism as boys tend to be.

I actually find boys more fun to teach! They are less concerned with doing the right thing and more with knowing what it is: less worried about getting the right answer and more interested in asking the right questions. We need to look carefully at why boys achieve significantly lower results in Key Stage 3 English, why many more of them end up in lower sets for certain subjects, and why the national trend towards fewer boys achieving A–C grades is continuing in selected subjects. It has everything to do with self-esteem and nothing whatever to do with natural potential.

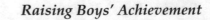

Section Four

Biological Factors

Advanced Organiser

☛ **Girls' brains equip them to be better linguistically; boys' brains to be better at visual-spatial activities.**

☛ **Girls' brains are better suited for current systems of assessing achievement.**

☛ **The issue is too complex for simple solutions based either on genetics or the environment.**

☛ **Boys can be helped to analyse and girls can be helped to speculate.**

1 Cause

This is one of the most controversial areas of the debate on boys' underachievement. It is essentially an argument between those who see achievement as the result of people's genetic make-up and those who claim that people's upbringing is by far the most significant factor in developing people's learning potential. And people have very strong views one way or another about it!

For the first part of an activity, try to ask 20 adults (10 men and 10 women) and 20 pupils (10 boys and 10 girls) the following:

> Which is more important in deciding whether people become successful learners or not – what they are born with or what they develop because of the way they are brought up?

Respondents have to opt for one or the other. At a pinch you might allow 'don't know', but try to discourage this. The question is not meant to be answered as the result of informed discussion, so just ask it and get them to plump for one answer or the other. (If you have young children aged under seven or eight in your class, this might be difficult but not impossible if you can phrase the question appropriately.) When you have finished make a simple table to record the results and keep them for later use.

		% age Yes	% age No	% age Don't Know
Adults	Men			
	Women			
Pupils	Boys			
	Girls			
All	Total			

What exactly is the debate about? Extensive research carried out by Geoff Hannan, an educational trainer, into the main arguments suggest that geneticists would claim that about two-thirds of a person's capabilities are predetermined by our genes, and are unalterable by any background factors.

This explains why most girls/women have more effective eyesight, better peripheral vision and greater sensitivity to low light. On the other hand, boys/men have better stereoscopic vision and see better in sharp light. Girls/women have more sensitive hearing, smell and taste than boys/men. And, crucially for our purposes, they have more developed areas of the brain that deal with linguistic intelligence, whereas boys/men have highly developed visual-spatial centres in their brains. The male is better at mental rotation, while the female is better at verbal fluency. In other words ...

Stimulus Quotation 9

"He's better at reversing a car. She's better at telling him how to do it. He has a mindset 'I think'. She has a mindset 'I feel'. He polarises. She holisticises."

from **Improving Boys' Performance**, Hannan G (Inset Materials, 1996)

There is considerable scientific evidence and assertion in this area, which claim that females are more analytical and reflective in their approach to learning, because of the areas of their brain which are more highly developed. Conversely, males are more speculative and experimental around their learning, because of the highly developed areas in their brains. Given the current assessment system in the UK, which is based on a sequential and analytical approach to learning, girls are advantaged considerably.

Left Brain

language
logic
mathematical formulae
number
sequence
linearity
analysis
words of a song
learning from the part to the whole
phonetic reading system
unrelated factual information

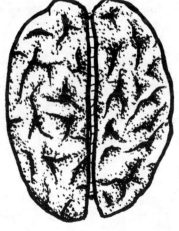

Right Brain

forms and patterns
spatial manipulation
rhythm
musical appreciation
images and pictures
dimension
imagination
tune of song
learns the whole first then parts
daydreaming and visioning
whole language reader
relationships in learning

from **Acclerated Learning**, Smith A (Network Educational Press, 1996)

But environmentalists would argue that people's learning propensities are less the result of genetic imprinting, and more the result of the way they are brought up – Geoff Hannan's nurture theory. Evidence about boys' reading preferences would be a good example of this. Recent research in this field with over 400 pupils aged 10 to 12 concludes that boys' reading choices are determined generally very much by what they see other people reading, and this includes adults and peers as well as other boys and men. It may be that they like to read action, adventure or horror material, but this research showed that girls liked these reading stimuli as well. Nearly 50 per cent of boys liked these sorts of books, but 40 per cent of girls said they also liked them.

But, crucially, this was not uniform across the six schools in the research. There was a huge difference amongst the schools, not just in the types of books boys and girls liked to read, but also in the amount of reading that they did. In some schools the boys 'outscored' the girls in their frequency and enjoyment of reading: in others they were roughly the same, and in some they were behind.

The single most significant factor appeared to be the impact of the teacher on their enthusiasm about reading. The boys – and girls! – responded to the model of reading which the teacher presented to them, and this seemed to be more important to them in the classroom than what other boys read. Boys indicated also that they are influenced strongly by other models of adult readers, particularly their fathers.

What is clear is that there is no incontrovertible proof one way or the other. However, there is a clear recognition that the inter-relationship is a complex one. It also seems hard to deny that children are affected to some extent in their learning by the home and school context.

Stimulus Quotation 10

"The boys, consciously or otherwise, model some of their own reading behaviour on their fathers' particular reading styles and preferences. Perhaps their response to books, the kind of reader they are becoming, is closely related to their view of their fathers as readers."

from **Reading the Difference**, *Minns H (CLPE, 1993, ed Barrs and Pidgeon)*

There have long been arguments about which is more influential, the home or school, with the overall feeling being that it is the home background which is more significant. But, school effects are measured between 5 per cent and 15 per cent, depending on the effectiveness of the teaching. So the supporters of the 'nurture' theory would say that it is possible for boys' underachievement to be explained in terms of family background and/or school experience, especially if the measure of achievement is to compare boys with girls.

If, for boys and girls, the 'nature' explanation regarding different aspects of their brains is as much as 50 per cent of their potential to achieve, then surely the achievement of all, or most, girls, would be significantly better than all, or most, boys. That there is such great variety amongst the performance of boys and girls, in their many different schools in their many different settings, would seem to suggest that there is too little 'uniformity' amongst the genders to give much credence to the belief that genetics are the dominant factor.

2   Solution

If, for you, the 'biological' argument is a convincing one, then there would appear to be very little that schools can do to raise boys' achievement. If our learning potential and propensities are more or less fixed at birth, as a result of our gender, then boys are going to be disadvantaged from the outset. This is especially so if achievement is measured by an assessment or accreditation system which favours learning in one particular way.

But, because we know that people can learn things even in the most discouraging circumstances, we also know that it is not the switching of one brain type into another that is the answer. There is another way of approaching the problem, which looks to develop those skills and learning strategies which are not well developed at any given moment in time.

It is encouraging to see that the most controversial cause can produce the least controversial answer! Encouraging because it shows that complexity and simplicity are common aspects in the issue of boys' achievement, and that it may be that looking more at the complexity of individual cases will lead to the simple answers which fit them uniquely. The current obsession seems to be to look at educational issues the other way round, namely to try to find a simple, single cause to a complex problem and then come up with a generalised solution which fits everyone.

For those who advocate the 'nature' theory, it is recommended that there should be an 'evening up' of the current assessment and examination system, which in its present form favours a more 'girl friendly' sequential approach to learning. A system which allows for the more speculative and experimental approach of the boys, particularly with greater emphasis on 'terminal' examinations, would even up the overall balance which has switched dramatically since the mid-1980s following the introduction of curriculum and assessment changes such as GCSE, National Curriculum level descriptors, Key Stage assessments and modular elements in A Level examinations. It is thought that restoring the balance in assessment methods would help boys achieve better on a more even playing field. This theory is hotly-contested and not well-supported. There is more detailed discussion of this in *Section Seven*.

A more practical solution for schools is to leave the curriculum programme and assessment procedures alone and concentrate on the need to develop learning strategies in pupils to compensate for areas of learning weakness. And this applies to girls as well as boys! So for boys and girls there should be a systematic and sustained drive to encourage all pupils to think analytically and speculatively, and for them to try to recognise when it is appropriate to use one style, when it is appropriate to try another and when it might be sensible to use a variety.

Geoff Hannan has devised a helpful template which can be used in most subjects, to develop sequential and speculative thinking. The examples on pages 51 and 52 are for English and Science – subjects long thought to 'belong to' the different genders. This is largely because of the learning strategies these subjects seem to 'prefer', rather than any link to gender identity. For pupils and English (a 'girls' subject') he suggests a five-step approach to story writing. This is to develop in pupils a step-by-step thinking process, which analyses steps rather than getting to the end as soon as possible. The process should be talked through with a partner first, affirming the link between oracy and literacy.

The English template aids drafting – a process used by many teachers already. It has the advantage of encouraging pupils to develop a story sequentially. First pupils have to reflect on what they want the story to be about, and then to think about aspects of character, setting and emotions at the beginning and end of a story, and to consider the language which might be appropriate to use during the story.

Writer's Note Sheet

I want to show or explore ...

1. My story starts like this :

    _____
    _____
    _____
    _____

    Describe the scene:

    The characters:

    Their feelings/mood:

2. Then this happens

    _____
    _____
    _____
    _____

3. Then this happens

    _____
    _____
    _____
    _____

4. Then this happens

    _____
    _____
    _____
    _____

5. My story ends like this :

    The scene:

    The characters:

    Their feelings/mood:

    Some interesting words and phrases I am going to use ...

    _____
    _____
    _____
    _____
    _____
    _____
    _____

Improving Boys' Performance, *Hannan G (Inset Materials, 1996 © Geoff Hannan. Full rights remain)*

Science Speculation Sheet

I want to find out:

_____
_____
_____
_____
_____
_____

I think that:

I can test this by:

Result:

_____
_____
_____
_____

I now think that:

I can test this by:

Result:

_____
_____
_____
_____

I now think that:

I can test this by:

Result:

_____
_____
_____
_____

I have discovered that:

_____
_____
_____
_____
_____

Improving Boys' Performance, *Hannan G (Inset Materials, 1996 © Geoff Hannan. Full rights remain)*

Raising Boys' Achievement

As to a speculative approach, Geoff's example is from science (a 'boys' subject'). Here pupils have to consider a more experimental approach to learning, by a trial-and-error process.

Clearly it is advisable to try to use the two approaches across the subjects to encourage different forms of thinking within them, and Geoff Hannan has examples of these. His advice to teachers is always not to worry about believing him, but to try the methods and see what happens. So whatever your contacts are with children, at whatever age, try each method as required with a group of boys and girls whom you teach. The key is to make sure that the pupils have to sustain the approach over each stage, so that substantial sequencing or speculating has to take place. Note carefully any differences in boys' and girls' capability to deal with both methods – and choose which method(s) might be best suited to a piece of work.

Finally... go back to the 20 adults and the 20 pupils to whom you asked the question about 'nature' and 'nurture' earlier on. Talk to them about the information from the opposing camps. Then ask both groups of people to answer the question again. You may find the 'nurture' camp increases its percentage of the vote, even if it does not 'win' overall.

Case Study Three 3

Hartcliffe School, Bristol

This report about after-school activities in a secondary school situated on a large Bristol housing estate was written by the teacher-in-charge, Vic Ecclestone. A fuller version appeared in the Winter 1996/1997 edition of 'Ninety-Five Per Cent'.

My involvement in after-school activities really started when I was approached by a group of 14 year-olds who wanted to play cricket and thought, somewhat naively, that this should be a fairly easy problem to solve. Several telephone calls later, I began to realise that the situation was not going to be simple. The school grass wicket had been built on, the artificial wicket had a piece cut out of it that looked suspiciously like a back door mat and the nets were growing beans somewhere on the estate. This was coupled with little kit, no coaches and the removal of the indoor cricket nets by the local sports centre.

I phoned John Budd at Bedminster Cricket Club who thought the whole idea of coaching cricket at Hartcliffe so crazy that he helped immediately. He ended up coaching 22 young men on a five-a-side court at the local sports centre. With the addition of a regular coach this increased to 96 young men and women. This developed against a background of 'Hartcliffe children wouldn't'. They couldn't be depended on.

The programme was slowly expanded. Outdoor pursuits became a regular feature, canoe-training took place and by now over 200 young people were taking part in regular after-school practice. The Sports Council moved in a half-time co-ordinator to help. With the arrival of help I could now concentrate on the Arts and we all know Hartcliffe children wouldn't like opera!

I phoned Welsh National Opera and, three weeks later, *Macbeth* was performed in the school hall in front of a hundred and fifty 11 year-olds. Workshops followed. Then followed visits and workshops by D'Oyly Carte Opera Company, Rambert Dance, Royal Opera House, musicians, composers and a range of performance companies keen to share their expertise. It was at one of the Rambert Dance workshops, which was all girls, that I got talking to a group of older boys hanging round the door. 'Why can't we dance?' Why indeed, I thought ... I knew I would only have one chance to make a male dance project work. If I got it wrong it would take years to repair the damage. The dance project could, if organised and presented badly, wipe out any developing self-confidence among the young people.

Shortly after the riots in Hartcliffe I approached the Birmingham Royal Ballet and suggested that we might work on a project involving 40 boys. The girls involved would produce the technical side of the performance, lighting plan, research programmes and so on. Evan Williams led the four-day residency to produce *Bigger the Bump*. This was a piece that drew comparisons between boxing and dance. It was performed in front of parents and friends and the curious on the estate. Standing ovation. After that, there was no looking back. We now have about 40 boys and young men who dance on a regular basis. They are led by Chris Lewis-Smith who has produced four new pieces for them to dance.

One of the pieces is *As You Are*, based on some of the issues in the life of Kurt Cobain. All the students took part in a number of workshops focusing on a variety of concerns – drug addiction, loss, family break-up and growing up. Their thoughts and feelings were then built into the dance–theatre piece and professionally filmed. It has now been performed in a variety of locations and as part of the 50th anniversary celebrations of the United Nations. During the International Festival of the Sea, 25 young men performed a work in front of an audience of two thousand, and are now selecting music from Massive Attack for a new piece to perform early in 1997. Recently, two hundred 10 and 11 year-old boys from the area took part in workshops with the Royal Ballet.

All this is not about producing dancers for dance school – if that happens, brilliant, but it is not the core of the work. We found that these young people were viewed by many outside the estate in a totally negative way: Hartcliffe children wouldn't – wouldn't want cricket, wouldn't want opera, music, dance. We have proved this view wrong with a vengeance.

Secondly, it is about introducing young people to a whole series of practical things: Where is the theatre? How do you use a ticket? Where and when do you clap? No, you can't eat crisps during the show. Many of our young people are disbarred from mainstream culture for a variety of practical reasons.

It is also about fun, self-image and doing something well: our emphasis is two days of excellence, not four weeks of mediocrity.

The young people here learn too that creating a production is very hard work, physically and mentally. Now when they see a performance they have some understanding of the whole process. This increased self-confidence has spilled over from the after-school programme into other areas of school life. Opera school now happens in the summer holidays; acting schools during Christmas and Easter breaks are full; a large choir has been formed and a junior section of the Boys' Dance Company is opening after Christmas. Nor is it just dance. To date, the Royal Shakespeare Company, Royal Opera House, Welsh National Opera, English Ballet, Adventures in Motion Pictures, Rambert Dance Company, painters, composers and a whole variety of artists have visited, helped and inspired our young people.

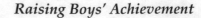

Section Five

The School Influence on Boys

> **Advanced Organiser**
>
> ☛ **Do boys need male role models in schools or good teacher role models?**
>
> ☛ **There is some support for boys' perceptions that they get picked on.**
>
> ☛ **The stature of all adults in schools needs to be raised.**
>
> ☛ **Teachers need to be aware of the ways in which they deal with boys and girls.**

1   Cause

There are two strands to this area of concern. The first strand is that boys have too few male teachers as role models, particularly in primary school, and this gives them a negative view of schooling. The second strand is linked to a widely-held perception of boys that they are 'picked on' unfairly by teachers, and that this contributes to a number of them switching off in school and, eventually, to some of them dropping out altogether from secondary school.

Strand 1: Male Role Models

There is a point of view in the UK that boys' underachievement can be linked to the fact that many boys come into contact mainly with women in their formative years . This, the argument continues, has a detrimental effect on boys' educational development, because boys are not able to see role models of successful men at home and in school. At home this is seen in single-mother families. In an educational context, this is exacerbated by the female world of the primary school. There is a sinister aspect to this strand, namely that the largely female world of the home and primary school is to 'blame' for the relative underachievement of boys.

The assumption is that what boys learn at primary school, how they learn it and who they learn it from, impacts on their learning negatively in comparison with girls, simply because the environment is largely a female one.

> **Stimulus Quotation 11**
>
> "... it is likely that the lack of close contact with male role models at a more everyday level, such as male readers in the classroom give the reading process (and with it the whole school process) the air of a feminine sphere of influence, and that of a lowly kind in the eyes of the boys."
>
> from **Reading the Difference**, Hodgeon J (CLPE, 1993, ed Barrs and Pigeon)

This argument has been developed in the USA by educators like Stephen Holland, who has advocated male mentors for black boys in order to compensate for a female-dominated school environment. He believes that the underperforming of black boys is due in large part to the lack of adult black male role models, particularly in schools. As a result, he helped establish an in-school mentoring programme called Project 2000. Its successes, and those of similar programmes it has spawned, may be due in part to the male mentor.

But, whatever advantages it may have, people see a potential downside to this model. It may also succeed in reinforcing a notion of gender superiority, namely that being taught by a woman is an inferior experience to being taught by a man. It may be that the use of mentors, male and female, may be a useful strategy, but it is only one amongst many other strategies which have to be considered carefully. As to the best strategies ...

Stimulus Quotation 12

"Such strategies do not make simplistic assumptions about women teachers' incapacity (including black women) to educate black boys purely on the basis that women have been totally devalued in the eyes of the boys, as a result of the subordination of women in society as a whole."

View from the Front Line, *John G (© The Guardian, 26.09.95)*

The possibility that a female-dominated upbringing and education is detrimental to boys' achievement is an interesting theory. But is it just that – a theory ? Perhaps there is something to the view that primary classrooms, with their emphasis on stories, fiction and predominantly female models of learners, suggest to children that learning is more likely to be a girl's activity than a boy's activity. But, it would be equally justifiable, from a theoretical standpoint, to suggest that adult males do not necessarily make the best role models for boys. An article by Parry in *The Guardian* – 'What's sex got to do with it?' (05.09.96) – outlines research from the Caribbean which suggests that some male teachers tend to reinforce attitudes which contradict the academic ethos of schools and that some perpetuate stereotypical attitudes about gender learning identity. As always in cases like this, it is useful to go to the boys themselves to see if they can shed light on the issue.

Ask a group of boys to note down individually in one column which words they would use to describe a good teacher, and in a second column which words they would use to describe a bad teacher.

Good Teacher	Bad Teacher
Firm	Makes you copy all the time
Interesting	Talks too much
Explains things	Can't control class
Friendly	Moans a lot
Fun	Shouts

If your boys are too young to do this activity in any great detail, you could read out a list of 20 words or so, and ask them to say whether the characteristics belong to a good or a bad teacher. You might find it better to ask young boys to record on to a cassette words to describe good and bad teachers, and then transcribe what they say. Do the words give you any clue as to the gender of either the good or the bad teacher? If you want to, you can do the same exercise with the girls to see if they reveal anything at variance with the boys. Usually they don't, but try it all the same.

Then, ask the pupils to draw pictures which show the characteristics of the good teacher and the bad teacher. A quick sketch in a classroom setting will be perfectly adequate. The crucial thing to note is whether the drawings are male or female, and, if so, which? In my research there seems to be no rhyme or reason to this, other than the usual association of the drawing with an actual teacher, who fits most of the characteristics above.

You could of course simply ask the pupils if they think men or women make better teachers, but this is something of a leading question. If you do, be sure to follow this up and ask them to explain what they mean by giving you concrete examples.

Strand 2: Boys get picked on by teachers more than girls

There is a stereotypical image of a typical boy – put upon, chip on shoulder, unwilling to accept criticism, blaming others for his misfortunes and loathe to engage in meaningful dialogue with adults. There is some observed truth in this. A group of Year 11 and Year 12 boys writing about the reasons for boys' underachievement, managed to come up between them with nearly 40 different reasons – only two of which apportioned any blame to boys themselves!

A concern about 'unfair' treatment is quite strong amongst many boys. They see teachers, both men and women, as more easy going with girls and far more likely to intervene with boys. Teachers tend not to be receptive to this point of view. Most of them, if asked, would say that boys are more disruptive than girls, they are much harder work and, to put it bluntly, they usually deserve any 'telling off', because they are messing about and/or not working!

But two recent pieces of research seem to suggest that the boys might have a point. One focuses on the different treatment of boys and girls by teachers. The other confirms these findings, and suggests that boys and girls are aware of the differences and understand why some boys come to resent it. Both of these are worth 'testing' by using one activity in your own classroom(s). You will need to have a colleague's support either to observe you teaching or to be observed by you. This can be difficult to arrange, taking up valuable non-contact time but is an extremely interesting activity to do. Indeed, without this research, there is a strong chance that you will not understand fully the impact of classroom interactions on boys and girls as learners, as seen through the pupils' eyes. It would be like doing a jigsaw without all the right pieces. You might well end up with an interesting enough picture at the end, but it would not be as reliable and informative as the real one!

The activity ties in with research work done by Marie La France in the USA in the mid-1980s. She explored the differential experiences for boys and girls in school through classroom observation of teachers' interaction with pupils.

What she found was that teachers, both men and women, were more positive overall in their dealings with girls than with boys. This, she claimed, operated both on a conscious

---

and a sub-conscious level, regardless of how fair a teacher was trying to be. It could take the form of teachers being less patient with boys, ignoring their attempts to take part in activities, or blaming them disproportionately for misdemeanours. Boys tended to be cajoled publicly into working whereas girls were 'nudged' into their work.

Interestingly, La France concluded that this was bad for both boys and girls: boys, because they come to be expected to be self-reliant and less in need of support, and girls, because they are discouraged from taking risks and being active learners.

Stimulus Quotation 13

"When female students are nudged into passivity, dependency, and silence rather than activity, autonomy, and talk, then the touch is anything but helpful."

from **Gender and Education Vol.3, No.1,** *La France M (Carfax, 1987)*

A focused observation of you by a colleague, or vice versa, can be set up and recorded quite easily. Remember that you are looking to see if boys are 'picked on' more than girls. In an all-boys school, you can do the same activity, by deciding in advance of an observation who are the working boys ('non-boys' in the other boys' eyes) and who are the non-working boys ('the lads'). Decide mutually how you are going to record pupil behaviour and teacher intervention. Make up a list of categories of behaviour that can be recorded accurately, and note what happens and when it happens. Note also whether there was any teacher intervention (T) and what form the intervention took - 'nudge' (TN) or 'loud challenge'(TLC).

Behaviour/Intervention Observation Form

Subject.. Year Group ....
Date and Time .... Teacher ....

No of Boys........ No of Girls........ Total..........

Behaviour	Boys	All	Girls
Calling out/Shouting			
Leaving Seat (with negative intent)			
Arguing with Teacher			
Arguing/Fighting with Each Other			

Tick each instance of disruptive behaviour and then note after it a brief explanation of what the behaviour was, when it happened, and, if there was teacher intervention, whether it was a 'nudge' (TN) or a 'loud challenge' (TLC).

Clearly a one-off observation may not give you enough evidence on which to base any serious theory, so you should try to do this more than once with your colleague. Share your findings as you go, so that you have two different perceptions about what seems to be happening. This 'feedback' may help you also to consider if you want to shift the focus at all, by targeting a group of boys, or one or two boys, or to change the categories in which you are going to observe them. If you can only afford the time to do one more observation, then do it within two or three weeks of the first one. This will allow enough distance between observations for the different interpersonal factors to be seen, allowing you comparison of the initial findings. But you will be close enough in time, not to have forgotten some of your original thoughts about the individuals and groups which you have focused on.

This may seem a slow, academic sort of activity, begging the questions, 'What is this showing us?'and 'How is this going to help my practice now?' Be patient, and stick with it, because it does pay dividends. This is because it is making you as a teacher look seriously at the learning that goes on in your classroom. This will reveal things which you cannot see alone, things which are both good and bad practice. It is part of that vital need to reflect on practice, but in a way which is focused sharply on boys – your boys – in real classrooms – your classrooms. And talking about learning in this way supports teachers and informs teaching.

At the end of what should be a limited research period, you will need to consider your findings carefully. The key factors are, first, the percentage of incidents of disruptive behaviour of boys and girls (adapting this for the target groups in an all-boys school) during the observation time, and, second, the percentage of teacher interventions made to these disruptions. You can do the overall figures first and then break them down into 'nudges' and 'loud challenges'. These findings can be compared with the subjective view you and your colleague will have of the observations. Do the 'results' seem to fit in with the way you felt the boys and girls behaved and worked? Or do the 'results' seem to indicate that there might be other factors at work?

Consider how your findings of one another at work with boys and girls, or different groups of boys, support or challenge La France's conclusions. Do we, as teachers, tend to nudge girls and challenge boys loudly because of something in us rather than because boys and girls behave very differently? I heard one teacher saying that she thought that most teachers are 'nicer' to girls, because, even when they do misbehave, they do so in a much more compliant way! Maybe there is some truth in this. Possibly boys are louder, more assertive, less concerned about teachers' authority than we would like them to be. This can challenge teachers' self-confidence and composure, making them far more determined perhaps to put down publicly the first sign of trouble from a known troublesome boy or group(s) of boys.

This brings us to the second piece of research. Using the above lesson observation format, Pickering carried out some research with Year 7 boys in a mixed comprehensive school in south-east London in 1996. Extended observations and subsequent discussions with pupils and teachers supported La France's conclusions that boys and girls are treated disproportionately severely, given the levels and frequency of their disruptive behaviour in the classroom. Both boys and girls are aware of this difference.

Just under 200 pupils (53 per cent girls – 47 per cent boys) were observed in 36 one hour lessons. Three categories of serious disruptive behaviour were looked for and recorded.

	Boys	Girls
Moving around Class (disruptively) (73 instances)	48%	52%
Shouting/Loud Talk (126 instances)	40%	60%
Arguing with Teacher (18 instances)	28%	72%
Total per cent Age of Disruptive Behaviour	42%	58%

These figures may not be typical of other schools, and they may not be representative of this particular school, given the relatively small scope of the research. But there was an awareness amongst teachers that they did sometimes have different expectations of boys and girls, and that this influenced the way in which they reacted to poor behaviour or lack of/poor quality work. This could operate at an almost sub-conscious level.

All the teachers whose lessons were observed were aware of the focus of the research, yet on more than one occasion individual teachers recognised afterwards that they had reacted to incidents in the class differently depending on the gender of the pupil(s). Indeed one extremely effective teacher said to the researcher after a lesson, 'I did it, didn't I ?' Asked to explain, the teacher said, 'I did it, didn't I ? I told the boys off more!'

This research supported La France's conclusions. But more than this, the follow-up discussions with pupils showed that there was a clear awareness of the different treatment of boys and girls. Some Year 11 boys, interviewed to give a retrospective perspective on changes in attitudes to school, said that they were aware of different treatment as far back as Year 4 or 5 at primary school. This tended to take the form of teachers spending more time helping girls with their work, with boys expected to know what to do and just to get on with things. If a boy asked for help, it was assumed that he just hadn't listened to the instructions properly.

But at primary school level this had been a source of annoyance, nothing more. By the early years of secondary school this had developed, for some of them, into a genuine sense of grievance, a feeling of unfairness. This was confirmed by several Year 7 girls in the school who said that some of the boys did tend to get blamed for disruption in a more public way then girls. They admitted also that they were not surprised that the boys got told off more for doing less in the way of disruption. The girls said that they were much more aware of – and concerned about – the position of the teacher in the classroom than the boys seemed to be. Accordingly, they tempered their behaviour to the likelihood of teacher intervention, and developed codes and signals to warn one another of possible problems.

It is very tempting to put these two school-based factors together and see some kind of causal link. If boys feel picked on unfairly in school from an early age it might be because of primary school, where girl learners are favoured by mainly female teachers. This would give boys a distorted view of school and encourage a growing sense of resentment at the unfairness. This might be avoided if there were more male teachers, or male role models, in primary schools.

2   Solution

We are all influenced by those around us, sometimes for the good and sometimes for the bad. If you ask an adult to name two or three of the important influences on their lives, and why they were so influential, they will usually say .....

..... Well, go on, ask them! And when they have told you who they were and why they had such a significant impact, ask them if the gender of the people was important in their choices. The likelihood is that it is what these people did, rather than their gender, which was important. The same seems to be true for children. They will pick up models which create gender stereotypes, but they will respond to all successful role models. They can also distinguish between good and bad aspects of role models. During recent concerns about the suitability of professional footballers as role models for boys, many of the boys interviewed said they liked footballers for their playing ability, but were less positive about some of the other personality traits they see reported in the media.

The strategy to deal with both strands of the school influence is to deal with the root causes of the unfair treatment, not to provide more male role models. Crucially, this is because one of the key findings of La France's and Pickering's research was that male teachers are just as 'guilty' of picking on boys as female teachers are. There is little point providing more male teachers at primary school level if they are going to pick on boys equally as often as their female counterparts. What might be more productive is to consider not the percentage of females in schools, but rather the role of those females compared with males in schools, particularly at primary level. Children come into contact with many adults, teachers and non-teachers, during the school day, and they see men and women taking up all kinds of roles.

Take a look at your own school(s). List the staff, teaching and non-teaching, full time and part time. Put them into categories such as management, classteachers, classroom support, premises, clerical and ancillary staff. You may not need to go very far with this before you know the answer to the question 'Do men or women make up the higher percentage of the 'senior' positions?'

If you are in a primary school, try comparing your findings with a local secondary school, and vice versa. Even if the balance is slightly different, is the overall picture still the same? In terms of status, as constructed by children, what are the male and female role models which they see? Is what the children, and indeed what many parents and 'outsiders' see, as described in Stimulus Quotation 14 (see over)?

Stimulus Quotation 14

"In Bankside School, parents cannot fail to notice the pattern of management of a large number of females, which is typical of many primary schools. It is a very simple situation. A large group of women, of whom a substantial number are ancillary workers, are bound into what King (1978) called a 'tight but authoritarian atmosphere' by a tiny number of men ..... Parents are less familiar with a male presence in the normal classroom. Neither the head or deputy has any teaching commitments, and so the children see them both as only authority figures, or the person who tells a story in assembly."

from **Reading the Difference,** *Hodgeon J (CLPE, 1993, ed. Barrs and Pigeon)*

It is going to be difficult to change the status of many of the females in schools, but it might be possible to work with colleagues on changing the status which they have in the eyes of the pupils. Indeed, the really successful strategy may not be to present boys with male role models, but to present them in schools with more successful female role models. These should not just be those women who are in positions of authority, but also those women who come into frequent contact with boys in a perceived 'lowly position'.

There are many assertiveness courses which can help teachers and ancillary staff be more positive personally in the role which they have. However, it might be more interesting and more beneficial for schools themselves to look at ways in which they can promote all staff as the models which pupils can look up to. The key way to do this is for adults to present themselves to pupils as successful promoters of learning – and this can be done regardless of gender.

As to the question of unfair treatment of boys, the solution lies clearly in teachers' increased awareness of the way they go about classroom interactions. Sometimes it takes another pair of eyes in classrooms, a critical friend, to point out where a teacher might be making a mistake – as well as doing things well, which a colleague can try out.

Case Study Four

Geoff Hannan, Educational Trainer

Geoff Hannan has been running a training and consultancy business for nearly 20 years, after a teaching career in which he had been a Deputy Headteacher. He is regarded widely as one of the leading experts (if not the leading expert) currently on boys' underachievement. He has written and trained all over the UK, Europe and the USA. This appreciation is written by the author who attended one of Geoff's training sessions in 1996.

All teachers and schools are aware of far too many school improvement efforts which have started in a flush of excitement, enthusiasm and commitment, only to run out of steam quickly and come to nothing. All too often this has happened after teachers have been 'out', individually or collectively, on in-service training, or after a consultant has been 'in', inspired teachers and then gone.

Frequently, the blame for this can be attributed to the fact that schools rarely have the time and/or the resources to pick up on the stimulus in a sustained and sustainable way; occasionally, it is because the ideas in the training are too generalised and do not fit in with the school's particular context; and, sometimes it is because the claims of the training or the consultant are over-hyped and unattainable. The problem with this is that it can often colour negatively teachers' views about the value of INSET, trainers and consultants. And yet, we all know how influential a good trainer can be, by providing inspiration, information, an outside view, and if you are lucky, a structured package, which combines theory and strategy.

Fortunately for those of us interested, in and committed to, raising boys' achievement, Geoff Hannan belongs to the influential category, highly influential indeed. In looking through his promotional literature again recently, I was struck by the boldness of the claims in it. But I was not in the least tempted to regard it as 'over the top'. What, for instance, does he say about an intensive full-day training programme for teachers, headteachers, LEA staff? Well, it will provide participants with:

✔ an in-depth understanding of gender differences, centred on the learning needs of boys and a detailed analysis of the reasons for their underachievement

✔ a range of whole-school approaches for improving boys' performance; including simple and effective data-based monitoring and line-management support systems

✔ a wide range of learning and behavioural management strategies for the classroom

✔ cross-curricular ideas for the teaching of central study, learning and thinking skills

✔ whole school and specific guidelines for the delivery of excellence in equal opportunities practice

✔ ways ahead ... a step-by-step guide to easily manageable whole-school development for improving the performance of boys

Some claims! But on the day I attended training, he managed to achieve all of this comfortably and left us all inspired. As mentioned earlier, this can be dangerous for schools where initiative overload is the order of the day. It is all very well to inspire teachers so that they want to use information and strategies to develop practice, but these can fall flat either when colleagues 'smile' at yet more good INSET ideas or when the day-to-day operational needs simply overwhelm the good intentions.

This can be all the more problematic when the communication of the training ideas are as powerful and stimulating as Geoff's is. The promotional literature is not overstating his effect when it quotes a *Paris Soir* entry: 'Rarely do we see someone with Geoff Hannan's powers of communication: an actor, comedian, writer and expert combined to enthral everyone from the grey-haired professors in the stalls to the pink-haired punks in the balcony'.

Yet this is not an issue for people who attend Geoff's training, as long as they remember that there is far more to him than the performance. The presentation is a bonus, whether it is to professionals out of the school setting, in schools to teachers or to pupils and parents. But it is there to serve the structure and systems, which will help schools to develop strategies to raise boys' achievement – not as an overnight sensation, but as part of a sustained initiative over a long period of time.

The key to Geoff's success as a trainer lies in the back-up systems and where these systems come from. As the promotional handout says, his 'training is rooted in the appreciation that good teacher INSET is about presenting ideas and strategies that are readily and easily used in the classroom and in whole-school development'. The disk which he provides is full of sound and interesting information such as prompts for discussion, databases for storing diagnostic data or learning objectives, and management training ideas. The disk is an indispensable tool for schools who become involved in initiatives to raise pupils' achievement, especially boys. Given the difficulty of getting Geoff's personal services quickly, because of the demand for him, it is worth considering taking the disk as a stand-alone service. Whether it is the synopsis on reasons for boys' underachievement...

Oracy precedes literacy; closeness to family; assessment; and, expectations.

... or on strategies in secondary school;

Teacher-questioning strategy; a structured and pluralistic approach to group work; a sequential step-by-step approach to lesson structures; talking-through prior to written tasks; utilise the challenge potential of your subject; mixed ability in Years 7 & 8; sensitive behavioural management; communication with pupils & parents; teaching learning skills through template.

... there is an abundance of materials and strategies which you will be able to use as part of your initiative.

The Early Years

Talk boys through the operations they are engaged in – on the floor with the Lego set, or sitting with the computer game. Ask questions, get them to be reflective. Involve them in 'planning' activities prior to constructional activities. Praise them for neatness, precision and accuracy. Encourage them into and praise them for co-operation. Engage them in discussions about feelings. Encourage them to talk through anger. Teach them to be assertive rather than aggressive in response to their peers.

If there are things which seem unlikely, Geoff's advice is not to just believe him, but to try them. My advice also is to try them.

Raising Boys' Achievement

Section Six

Boys and Girls – Equality of Opportunity?

> ### Advanced Organiser
>
> ☞ **Girls are more adaptable than boys to changing employment patterns.**
>
> ☞ **Boys do not respond to objective generalised evidence.**
>
> ☞ **Boys do not respond well to encouragement to work hard at school in order to increase job opportunities.**
>
> ☞ **Boys respond well to personalised target setting.**

1   Cause

The impact in the UK of the equal opportunities initiatives and legislation, designed to break down gender barriers, took place during the late 1970s and throughout the 1980s. These led to girls/women working more assertively to challenge the assumed 'right' of boys/men to dominate education and the workplace, and, subsequently, to compete with men in job areas once thought to be the domain of men. In schools this saw rigorous efforts to show, for instance, how much boys dominate space in playgrounds and teachers' time in classrooms. At the start of the initiatives, classrooms were seen as microcosms of society at large, with male domination so normal as to be scarcely visible, but where the preferential treatment of boys was an almost invariable rule. A focus on raising girls' achievement in schools followed, so successfully, that by the early 1990s there was ...

> #### Stimulus Quotation 15
>
> "... a growing concern about boys' underachievement, which has possibly gained force as a defensive reaction to recently girl-focused equality initiatives and to increasing evidence suggesting that girls are not underachieving, compared with boys."
>
> from **Gender and Education Vol.5, No.1,** *Harris S, Nixon J and Rudduck J (Carfax, 1993)*

This catching up by girls led inevitably to a shift away from the traditional domestic and secretarial ambitions of most female school leavers and set them on a collision path with their male counterparts, precisely at that time when there was a diminishing employment market. Although there was much talk at the time of the 'New Man', there is evidence from North America (Weis L, 1990), Australia (Connell R W, 1989) and the UK (Riddell S, 1992), which shows that for many boys there was still a strong vision of male-dominant roles, whilst girls were attempting to challenge the status quo. Things have changed markedly, especially where girls' career choices are concerned.

Some boys, however, have not been as adaptable, opting for the theory that boys' superiority will out in the end and that they just need to do more of the same, but a little bit better. Meanwhile, a significant number of girls are now ...

Stimulus Quotation 16

"... developing more radical conceptions of their future lives, opting for non-traditional subjects and career paths and quite explicitly challenging the sexual division of labour in the family."

Politics and The Gender of the Curriculum, *Riddell S (Routledge, 1992)*

An activity which tests gender expectations about career paths can be extremely informative. It can be used as a piece of simple research, encouraging pupils to develop good research practice. But, more than this, it can help you individually, and the school collectively, to build up a picture of how adaptable and flexible different groups of pupils are nowadays, compared with their parents or grandparents. It will also help you determine whether the theory that boys are less adaptable than girls applies to your school. In an all-boys school, you could twin up with a local girls' school or simply ask the boys to think what jobs girls do when they leave school – based on real examples and not on what they think girls ought to do!

Ask pupils to think what job they might do when they are grown up. Ask them also to say which jobs they think that boys and girls might do. List them all. Can they be categorised into stereotypical men's and women's jobs?

Thinking about Careers

(A) What job might I do when I leave school?

1.   2.   3.

(B) What jobs do boys and girls do when they leave school?

Boys
1.   2.   3.

Girls
1.   2.   3.

SCORE 3 points for each first choice, 2 points for each second choice, and 1 point for each third choice. Add points to rank order job choices.

(C) What do they say that they are going to do when they leave school?

List the top five choices

	Boys	Girls
1		
2		
3		
4		
5		

Then get the pupils to ask parents, and/or grandparents, questions about girls' and boys' job expectations when they left school. Categorise them in the same way as the previous activity.

What jobs did boys and girls expect to do when they left school?			
List the top five choices			
Male parents/grandparents		Female parents/grandparents	
Boys	Girls	Boys	Girls
1.			
2.			
3.			
4.			
5.			

There are two interesting factors to draw out of this information. First, are there similarities between the two lists despite the gender difference of the respondents? It is assumed that there was much greater certainty about job destinations depending on gender before the equal opportunities initiatives. Men and women assumed that they would go into certain jobs.

Second, are there fewer 'crossover' jobs now, fewer blurred edges? It is assumed nowadays that there is an acceptance by men and women that they might do similar kinds of jobs.

Do your findings bear this out? Note especially if any of the four groups you asked to respond revealed a non-stereotypical selection of jobs? Given the research evidence quoted earlier, you would expect that the 'modern' girls would show a more adaptable approach.

2 Solution

Your results will support or challenge the notion of a significant shift in girls' attitudes to post-16 opportunities, just as it will indicate if there is a noticeable stagnation in boys' attitudes. Are the girls thinking ahead, planning for the ever-shifting job market of the next century? Are the boys stuck in a way of thinking which belongs to times long gone? Perhaps it is all too easy to create a 'general' picture, which does not point up the differences between individual pupils.

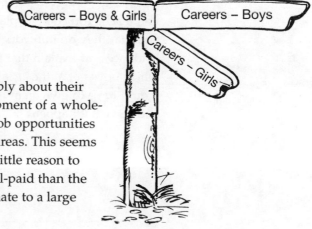

A suggested solution is to encourage boys to think more flexibly about their possible employment pathways. This would need the development of a whole-school approach, which presents boys with a wider range of job opportunities and ways of building up the skills needed to move into new areas. This seems to be something of an 'odd' strategy for many boys, who see little reason to move into non-stereotypical jobs, as most of them are less well-paid than the jobs which men have traditionally dominated, and still dominate to a large extent.

What this blanket view of female flexibility and male rigidity fails to take into account is the crucial social class dimension. The evidence from Connell, Riddell and Weis suggested that this male–female contrast was extremely marked in working-class areas, where men were reluctant to move away from the traditional attitudes of their parents and grandparents. The men did the work, the women looked after the family, and this included playing the key role in the children's education. The economic situation may have changed, but the old beliefs about male economic dominance, man as 'breadwinner', have remained largely unshaken. The recent development of a 'laddish' culture, with lads' comedians and lads' quizzes, bears testimony to the fact that achieving flexibility amongst boys and men may not be as easy as it seems, particularly with those from working-class backgrounds.

Stimulus Quotation 17

"It is, of course, at least theoretically possible that working-class men may seriously reconsider their own gender identity and even move into line with feminist thinking ... Given historic white-male dominance ... I am less than convinced that this is a possibility."

Working Class Without Work, Weis L (Routledge, 1990)

If traditional beliefs are more marked in working-class areas where traditional employment pathways have changed dramatically, this will be a harder nut for schools in these area to crack. But they exist to some extent in schools across the class divide. What could you try in your school, regardless of the scope of the problem?

It is well worth trying all three of the following strategies in your own school, applying your specific context to the national one. For instance:

> in (A) you might want to be looking at more local comparisons of the boys in your school with other schools in your area;
>
> in (B) you could look at gender employment patterns of your leavers compared with general trends in your region;
>
> in (C) you can consider if boys will – or already do – respond positively in your school to an individualised, action-planning approach.

Strategy A
Use reasoned argument and persuasion to look objectively at the evidence with boys you teach. You could explain to them that they do not work as hard as girls in school and that they do not work as hard at home on school work. Then show them all the evidence and explain that this has a dramatic effect on the test and examination results which boys get at the ages of 7, 11, 14, 16 and 18 in comparison with girls. Clearly you would have to give them the information relevant to their phase. Try it in a low-key way and see what happens.

For Key Stage 1 pupils		
At Level 2 or above	**Boys**	**Girls**
Reading	79%	88%
Writing	80%	89%
Mathematics	89%	91%
For Key Stage 2 pupils		
At Level 4 or above	**Boys**	**Girls**
English	70%	79%
Mathematics	82%	81%
Science	83%	84%
For Key Stage 3 pupils		
At Level 5 or above	**Boys**	**Girls**
English	55%	72%
Mathematics	64%	65%
Science	61%	59%

What about GCSE results in the core subjects? How can they help?

At GCSE level, these were the figures in 2000, as a percentage of all 16 year olds.

	Boys	**Girls**
Grades A* – C		
English	51%	66%
Maths	50%	50%
Science	49%	52%
All subject	44%	54%

Finally, there is the evidence of A Level results. This is what the 2000 figures show, as percentages of entries.

	Boys	**Girls**		**Boys**	**Girls**
Grades A & B			**Grades A-E**		
English	15%	19%		93%	94%
Mathematics	28%	20%		88%	91%
Biology	16%	21%		87%	91%
French	26%	21%		93%	92%

There are clear issues emerging from these figures, especially around the performance of boys in English. There is also the fact that girls do better in every GCSE subject with a large entry except Mathematics, where boys and girls do equally well. But the A Level results are interesting, showing a variety in performance, brought about by the fact that there is greater choice for A Level subjects than at GCSE. As the DfEE website says, 'when looking at A Level performance by gender in 2000 in terms of % getting A or B the picture is quite mixed, with boys outperforming girls in several subjects' and 'the gender gaps in success rates (% getting A–E) in these subjects is generally small'. The figures highlight two problems. First, the evidence is not convincingly damning of boys overall, with too much similarity and closeness. Second, it does not show what individual boys do, and is far too general to be useful in a localised, personalised context.

What did you find out? Were your boys convinced by the argument? If they were, then that is highly pleasing, and probably reflects your powers of persuasion, rather than the strength of the statistics. Research shows that boys are not particularly convinced by the 'objective' generalisation argument. Most boys can, and do, point to older boys who have done well at school, or to men who have done well in life despite a singular lack of success at school. The blanket argument tends to fail in the same way as trying to persuade smokers to give up, or fast drivers to stop speeding, because of the overall evidence of trends. We all know lots of people who are exceptions to rules! Even if you strike the right chord with one or two, you are unlikely to take all the boys with you on this one.

Strategy B

This strategy personalises things and attempts to convince boys individually that it is in their long-term interest to work hard, because a good job or, at least, better opportunities will come their way as a result. By all means try it. Even in the early years at primary school, children are surprisingly aware of the link between achievement at school and job opportunities later on.

But the trouble with this approach is that it flies in the face of all the current evidence about the proportions of men and women in different areas of the employment market. It is a regrettably long-standing fact that women may hold more than 50 per cent of the available jobs, but one-third of them earned under £190 per week in 1994 compared with one in eight men, because of the sort of jobs that they do. The incentive for boys to do well at school, in order to get the 'best' jobs, simply does not exist. The reverse may well be true, namely that girls have to work extra hard and do extra well in order to get some of the 'best' jobs, but that is not an argument to be followed to its logical end as far as convincing boys about the value of schooling is concerned.

It may have to do more fundamentally with entrenched prejudices about gender – and race – in the employment market. This can be considered in the area of homework, for instance. Here the relative importance which is attached to this by boys may come from a pragmatism about the status quo in the job market, and by girls to a desire to give themselves a better than even chance if they are to compete with boys on anything like equal terms.

Stimulus Quotation 18

"... it could well be the case that girls take their homework more seriously than boys due to their determination to do well academically ... They were determined to succeed, because they knew that the odds were stacked against them in terms of their race and gender."

Black Children and Underachievement in School, *Benskin F (Minerva Press, 1994)*

CAREERS INTERVIEWS

This is where it is possible to use role models, adult workers who show success in traditional and non-stereotypical areas. These should be men and women, so that boys and girls are exposed regularly to the wide range of opportunities available to them when they leave school. This should be done as experience of work in the workplace and of workers coming in as part of a planned programme.

Strategy C

The third strategy equips boys with the skills, techniques and knowledge to understand their learning and to apply themselves to it in a more structured and sustained way. This approach has links to three initiatives which approach a similar problem from different directions, and is concentrating the mind of many educational thinkers and politicians at the moment. The result is one of looking at pupil achievement in a less objective and generalised way, and focusing, through target setting, on the particular learning needs and achievements of the individual pupil.

Of the three possible strategies mentioned in this section this is the one which research shows is most likely to succeed with boys of all ages. It is highly successful with girls as well! As you work through this part, it would be illuminating for you to consider how much of this goes on in your school at present, how much of it is happening randomly or by design, and how much you could adapt to your own classroom or management practice immediately.

The first example comes from the systematic approach developed to improve the skills and knowledge of children with special educational needs. Enshrined now in the *Code of Practice and Assessment of Special Educational Needs* the clearly-stated objective of this approach is to improve educational experience by the provision for pupils of an individual learning programme. This is achieved by drawing up an Individual Education Plan.

Stimulus Quotation 19

"The SEN co-ordinator ... should ensure that an individual education plan is drawn up ... The plan should set out:

Stage 2 Individual Education Plan

- nature of child's learning difficulties
- action - the special educational provision
  - staff involved, including frequency of support
  - specific programmes/activities/materials/equipment
- help from parents at home
- targets to be achieved in a given time
- any pastoral care or medical requirements
- monitoring and assessment programmes
- review arrangements and date.

... The SEN co-ordinator should normally conduct the review ... The review should focus on:

- progress made by the child
- effectiveness of the education plan
- contributions made by parents at home
- updated information and advice
- future action"

Code of Practice on the Identification and Assessment of Special Educational Needs, *(DFE1994, Crown Copyright)*

Apart from the area of 'medical requirements', and this may still apply in individual cases, the template for working with individuals seems very close to many recently developed schemes which have sought to raise achievement by individual target setting and action planning for pupils.

This individual approach is seen in the second example, which focuses also on the learning needs of individual pupils, but at the other end of the attainment spectrum – highly able or gifted children.

Work with able children came initially from a parental frustration at the apparent failure of many schools to deal with some of its more able pupils. These are pupils who, despite their ability;

- tend to ask difficult questions
- are happy to talk a lot, but less inclined to write
- seem to be immature
- are pensive, but inattentive to allotted tasks
- get involved in high levels of displacement activity
- do not attain as well in school as out of it.

How many of your boys of all levels of attainment do you recognise here?

Now some schools, and one or two LEAs, have developed policies and strategies for exceptionally able pupils. They have moved away from a deficit model in which pupils are not achieving, to a proactive one, which, like the SEN Code of Practice, seeks to identify, work with and develop the individual needs of pupils.

Stimulus Quotation 20

"No two children – exceptionally able or otherwise – will have identical needs, not even identical twins! Very able children come from all sections of society and, like all children, will vary enormously in personality and outlook. They need to be regarded and treated as individuals from the start. Whatever their gender or ethnic group, the challenge is to ensure that all have an equal opportunity to fulfil their potential and develop as individuals."

Working with Very Able Children, *(City of Westminster, 1996)*

So it is possible to see the call to treat pupils individually extending to both ends of the attainment continuum, a move towards a partial sort of policy about learning. Some schools have taken this further and set up an overt policy for teaching and learning, focusing on pupil entitlement and strategies for effective learning.

Mention of effective learning leads into the third example. This stresses the role of records of achievement in raising the profile of individual achievement. There is little hard data to show that records of achievement *per se* have led to improved standards of achievement. However, there is a considerable body of evidence which points to the process bringing a more focused approach to the learning needs of individual pupils and the teaching strategies needed to raise achievement.

There are, of course, the direct impact of records of achievement linked to the procedures involved, namely recording, reviewing and reporting on achievement. Then there are indicators of indirect impact, through the increased motivation which pupils have gained from taking greater responsibility for their learning, the setting of clear objectives, a focus on learning and regular feedback. It is these indirect factors which most interest us when it comes to raising boys' achievement, as indicated in ...

Stimulus Quotation 21

"... we can point ... with some confidence to evidence that many pupils have found the opportunity of talking with their teachers on a one-to-one basis about achievements, experiences, needs and appropriate future targets a rewarding and helpful experience that has had a positive effect on their motivation."

Records of Achievement – Report of the National Evaluation of Pilot Schools, *Broadfoot P et al., (HMSO, 1988, Crown Copyright)*

But this detailed and rigorous evaluation highlighted several issues about records of achievement, two of which have been recurring themes in this book's attempt to focus your thoughts on how best to raise the achievement of your boys.

The first issue is that it is dangerous to make 'blanket' claims about the potential effectiveness which any given strategy may have on raising educational achievement. There is no blueprint to successful outcomes for all pupils, even if there may be common approaches which are worth trying. On increased pupil motivation the Record of Achievement National Evaluation noted: 'It is important, however, to qualify any such assertion with the proviso that pupils cannot be regarded as a homogeneous group in this respect. In records of achievement, *as in all other aspects of school life* (author's italics), pupils' responses reflect an immense diversity of personal and group characteristics such as personality, confidence, attitude, achievement level, gender, ethnic background and social class which combine in more or less idiosyncratic ways to colour their response to, and ability to profit from, such opportunities'.

The second issue is that it is not structures or systems but what happens in classrooms between individual pupils and individual teachers which is of greatest significance to increased and improved learning. On this, the evaluation said: ' It is clear from ... evidence that it is changes in classroom approaches and relations which underpin the impact on pupils. This is likely in turn to be a reflection of the extent to which teachers are genuinely attempting to institute not just a paper and pen exercise but a different approach to teaching and learning'.

If you are to take a strategic view of the problem, it would seem that an approach which focuses on setting targets for individual boys will have the best chance of success. The objective dispassionate parading of evidence about boys and/or the appeal to enlightened self-interest may have a few individual successes, but they will be limited. A partnership between teacher and boy-as-learner will be most productive. If the partnership can be embraced at whole-school level, or beyond, then the outcomes may be even more beneficial.

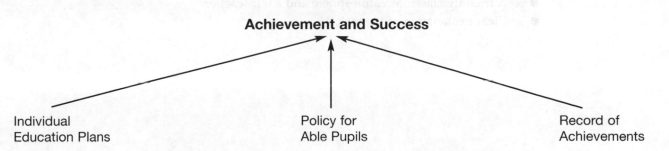

Achievement and Success

Individual Education Plans

Policy for Able Pupils

Record of Achievements

Raising Boys' Achievement

Case Study Five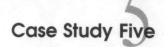

A Partnership Between Schools and a Local Education Authority

This case study shows the potential for partnership between schools and an external agency, their LEA. Three Dorset LEA inspectors worked with teachers from a first, middle and upper school in order to pool ideas about raising boys' achievement. This abridged account comes from the first draft of the report written by Harry Turner, the lead inspector, towards the end of the first year of the project. This format gives a clear idea of the methodology, initial findings, first conclusions, thoughts about possible strategies and further research possibilities.

Methods used

- Survey of National Curriculum Assessments, public examinations.
- Observations of boys in Years 3, 7 and 11.
- Focus group representative of ability range.
- Perception questionnaires for boys and girls.
- Classroom observations of the focus groups.
- Work survey of the focus group in English, Maths and Science.
- Interviews with focus group.

Notes

- Issues identified in this draft are common to three schools.
- Each school will have a separate report/discussion of specific issues for their school.
- The majority of identified issues and strategies are appropriate for girls and boys.

Issues to emerge

Evidence from questionnaires and interviews points to boys' high level of concern about their progress in school, their aspirations to improve and clear view of what they need to do to improve. The findings showed that 87 per cent of Year 3 boys think they can do better; 89 per cent worry that they do not always understand what the teacher wants. Year 7 boys identified the need to improve skills and knowledge in English and Maths to get a good job.

What helps pupils to learn?

- Work matched to ability.
- A friendly classroom atmosphere and a fair teacher.
- Clear explanation of the task.

How to improve pupils' work?

- Improving presentation.
- Improving English skills, especially handwriting, spelling and writing.
- Improving basic Maths skills.
- Development of study skills and attitudes to homework.
- Regular feedback on progress.
- Identifying next steps of learning.
- Seating arrangements.
- More opportunity for discussion, debate and sharing ideas.
- Greater use of speaking and listening activities to enhance learning and understanding.

Subject/activity likes and dislikes

- Girls are more inclined to identify core subjects as subjects they like.
- Boys prefer science, construction, playing games and making.
- High percentage of girls do not like problem solving and scientific investigations.

Strategies

1 Consistent approach to collection of performance data; use of this to classify broad achievement groups and to target support and work. For example: use of qualitative and quantitative data.

2 Target groups of pupils and provide opportunity to improve basic skills in English at an early stage.

3 Develop consistent approaches across schools which give high profile to pupils' learning in:
- presentation of work ● handwriting ● spelling ● improving writing skills

4 Develop opportunities for pupils at an earlier age to learn of careers and skills required.

5 Develop communication with parents outlining expectations of their involvement at various stages. This should cover:
- Listening to children read.
- Helping with tables and spellings.
- Giving clear expectations of homework.
- Outlining need for a study environment.
- The type of support needed in upper school.

Teaching and Learning

1 Raise awareness and develop practice in the following areas:
a) Clear expectations of tasks with visual reinforcement and opportunities for clarification questions.
b) Importance of prioritising the teaching of speaking and listening skills. Provide regular opportunities to practise these skills in lessons.
c) Collaborative work. Emphasis on joint work, sharing ideas, developing critical responses, teaching of social skills to support pair/group work.
d) Development of feedback strategies by the teacher to give value to and support for learning in lessons and clear information on individual progress and next stage of learning.

2 School's response to the development of consistent approaches to the management of pupils for learning. For example, developing a policy on seating arrangements for pupils.

3 Development of teaching programmes which identify learning skills at the various stages which will cover skills of planning, presentation, reviewing and improving. To include development of study skills and strategies of personal time and organisation management.

Raising Boys' Achievement

Section Seven

The Influence of Central Government Policy

Advanced Organiser

☞ **Girls do better than boys at coursework and examinations.**

☞ **Gender-stereotypical subject preference is not prevalent amongst boys or girls.**

☞ **Teachers are key to ensuring boys and girls are well prepared for assessments.**

☞ **Effective teaching is the key to raising achievement.**

1 Cause

It has been suggested that boys would have been just fine if there had been no introduction of GCSE examinations or a National Curriculum in the mid to late 1980s. Keeping the status quo – O Levels or CSE examinations at age 16 and a curriculum opted into by schools – could have been balanced by the equal opportunities initiatives mentioned in *Section Six*, in order to equalise girls' and boys' opportunities at school. But changing both the curriculum and assessment methods tipped the balance unfairly in the direction of the girls.

The introduction of the National Curriculum took away the opportunity for schools and pupils to specialise in areas of study most relevant and interesting to them. It did so by prescribing what pupils should study and restricting severely syllabus or topic choice by teachers and subject choice by pupils. Moreover it 'forced' pupils to study things which they did not particularly want, and for much longer. This meant inevitably, so the argument continues, that boys and girls ended up doing subjects that they did not enjoy and/or that they were not good at. For girls this opened up opportunities to compete with boys in subjects that had helped to give boys an immediate advantage into higher education and the workplace. The new requirements offered little in return to boys by way of 'better' educational or work chances.

At the same time the assessment and examination of the curriculum changed. There was, and still is, although to a lesser extent recently, an increased element of continuous assessment, and this favours the more sequential learning of girls (see *Section Four*). Terminal examinations count for less, and, even where examinations are important, there is greater grade reward for the ability to learn analytically and in stages, rather than the ability to speculate and experiment. For boys this has taken away that element of their learning identity which is a great strength, replacing it almost exclusively with an assessment system that suits girls' learning styles and strategies.

The activities in this section invite you to consider first, with the help of your pupils, what the evidence actually shows you as far as assessment is concerned. Then you will be able to consider some strategies which might support your attempts to improve standards of achievement, by working in a more informed way from within existing assessment procedures. Following that you will be able to explore with pupils the 'real' evidence about pupils' subject preferences and how these might inform the debate about boys' and girls' subjects. This will help you to consider whether pupils' subject disposition or effective teaching is more influential in raising achievement.

The activities will take some time to complete but will sharpen your understanding of the relationship between gender, pupil achievement and assessment requirements.

(A) Examinations and continuous assessment

Stimulus Quotation 22

"There is a widespread perception that girls' success in the GCSE can be solely accounted for by their success in the coursework elements of examinations. Further investigations into this issue at GCSE showed this not to be the case ...The same questions regarding gender, coursework and performance have been asked in relation to the A level ... What seems to be evident from the data ... is that coursework contributes less to the overall grade for females than it does for males. Females perform slightly better at coursework than males, but it is the examination papers than contribute most to their overall performance."

**Gender Differences in A Level Examinations:
the Reinforcement of Stereotypes,** *Elwood J and Comber C, (1995)*

Elwood and Comber go on to argue that outcomes are influenced also by the stereotypical beliefs about achievement and performance which are held in equal measure by teachers and pupils. Focusing unnecessarily on assessment issues will deflect attention away from the teacher–learner experience, which has been identified as the crucial aspect in efforts to raise boys' achievement.

What you can do in your own school is to test two things which Elwood and Comber highlight: the arguments about coursework and terminal examination; and the assumptions about the different subject preferences of boys and girls.

The first step could be to ask direct questions of your pupils:

> Do you prefer to do coursework or one-off examinations to show what you have learned? Or do you prefer a mixture of both? Try to explain your answer.

These questions will be suitable for older pupils in Key Stage 2 and beyond, but you will probably have to explain to some what coursework is. However, you will need to modify the questions for younger children. Try to frame some questions to see if they have a view about 'sitting-down' type tests, and to compare this with work that you, the teacher, mark in a formal way.

Whichever approach you use, it is useful for you to have the pupils' views about examinations and continuous assessment as your baseline evidence. You may well have your own preconceptions about this, and it is important that you take a joint learner–teacher perspective into these activities to minimise the possibility of prejudging issues and findings.

It is the differences and similarities between boys' and girls' views that will have been informative from the answers to the above question(s) (or any variety and sameness, if you are in an all-boys' school).

Armed with this information, you can then test empirically whether your pupils perform better or worse in formal tests/examinations or by continuous assessment. In your school or in your subject area you may already do something like this, but for many schools the process stops at evaluation *after* the event. The following activity is a proactive process, in order to inform you *before* the event, and to give time for strategies to be worked out and implemented.

This should be relatively easy to do, but it will take time. For some pupils you will already have results of Key Stage tests or GCSE/GNVQ examinations, and you can compare these results with teacher assessments or coursework marks. For other pupils it should not be too difficult to construct a brief test, or a series of brief tests, given the availability of past tests for pupils at Key Stages 1, 2 and 3, and previous papers at GCSE, GNVQ and A level.

Use the results to obtain a measure of the success of individual pupils and groups of pupils in an 'examination situation'. It is important that there is a strong sense of realism about this process, with pupils aware when the test(s) will take place and properly prepared. The assessment/marking of the test should be known in advance and the test itself should be done in properly explained examination conditions.

Once the test – or series of tests – is over, you can compare the scores with your ongoing, evidence-based teacher assessments about National Curriculum levels or predicted Year 11 and post-16 public examination grades. Then it will be possible to make comparisons about the relative performance of boys and girls, or different groups of boys.

How does your data compare with the Elwood and Comber findings? Is there significant gender difference, or is individual variety too wide to make generalisations by gender alone?

After the test(s) ask the pupils for some qualitative information about tests. The purpose is to gain insights into how the pupils feel about tests/examinations, in order to see if there is any match between attitudes to tests and successful examination technique. The test(s) will have given you valuable information, but will tell you only what pupils knew or could recall at that point in time. The test(s) will not tell you what led up to their performance in terms of approach and understanding, their thoughts and worries, the pressures on them at home or from friends, their ability to prepare, or the facilities available to help them prepare successfully.

You could design your own questions or use the following:

? Did you find the test easy? Why (not)?

? Did you understand what you had to do?

? Did you know all of the answers? If you did not, do you know why?

? Did you finish on time? If you finished early, why was this? If you did not finish on time, what went wrong?

? Did you feel calm during the test or did you want to panic at times?

? Did you get stuck on anything during the test? If you did, what did you do?

? Did you do any preparation for the test? If you did, explain what you did. If you did not prepare, why not?

? Are you worried about doing well in the test? Explain your answer.

? How will you feel if you have done badly in the test?

? What might help you to do better in the next test? Try to think of things which you could do and things which your teacher could help you with.

Qualitative information is important because you are not trying to make just a 'statistical' comparison between tests and coursework. You are also attempting to see what might be the underlying causes for any differences, which may help you to think about your boys' underachievement. Therefore, it is wise to consider what the pupils are saying about why they performed as they did in the test(s), not just what their scores or grades might tell you.

You should do the same activity with the same pupils about a piece or pieces of 'assessable' classwork, in order to have a comparison of their attitudes to coursework as well. You can ask virtually the same questions, simply changing the word 'test' to 'task', and altering the question about preparation to one about planning or drafting.

Remember that you are looking to build up an overall profile of each child which can feed into an overall profile of boys and girls and, if possible, sub-groups within them. A grid to write down brief notes could be helpful.

Pupil Name	Test Score(s)	Opinions on Tests	Continuous Assessment Levels	Opinions on Assessed Tasks

It is useful to return to the questions you asked after you have collected the 'hard' data from the test(s) and your own assessments and look at them again, now that you have some interesting qualitative information. You could add the views of the pupils, putting some flesh on the bones of the data which you compared in a general way with the Elwood and Comber findings. Then you can try to explain if there is a significant gender difference, or if the individual variety is too wide for you to make generalisations by gender alone. It might be useful to make a list of the different factors thrown up by the pupils' responses and to look at them in terms of frequency, nature and priority. Then reflect on the following questions before moving on.

? Does your evidence suggest that boys and girls differ in their success with continuous assessment or 'one-off' examinations?

? If so, is it consistent for all boys and all girls? Does the 'hard' data match the views of the pupils?

? If not, are there any recognisable patterns for groups of boys and/or groups of girls?

? Do the views of your pupils about coursework and examinations offer you any clues about why some of them may be successful in one or the other form of assessment, or both?

? If so, can you use this to help less successful pupils? How?

? If not, is there any further research you could do with your pupils, in order to learn more from your successful learners?

(B) Subject preferences

Stimulus Quotation 23

"In all year groups girls read more fiction books than boys and tended to have different tastes in reading ... Poetry was often less popular with boys than girls ... Boys made less use of school libraries than girls and took less part in English-related extra-curricular activities ... Girls wrote at greater length and generally received higher marks than boys for written work ...There were no obvious differences in the performance of boys and girls in spoken English ..."

Boys and English, *(OFSTED 1993)*

Much of the recent discussion about boys' underachievement has stressed the significant disparity between the examination performance of boys and girls in English. If we can accept now that this is not explained by the coursework issue, or at least not proven, then it has to be worth exploring the notion that it is linked to subject preference, either because of a gender issue or personal liking, or both. A 'gendered' preference or personal liking may affect to some degree the pupils' willingness to do well, their subject choices where subject choices are possible, and finally their test or examination results.

The activities here will ask you to look at your boys in order to see if there is a possible correlation between a gendered image of a subject and boys' achievements in it. The activities are straightforward, and can be done using the ten National Curriculum subjects.

Start by checking the views of adults in your school as the first step. Ask ten or twenty adults (easier for calculating percentages) to fill in the form below. Try to choose a reasonable balance of teaching and non-teaching staff to do this, simply to reflect the proportion of adult thoughts in the school.

Do you think that some National Curriculum subjects are boys' subjects and some are girls' subjects?

               Yes   **No**   **Unsure**   **(Please circle)**

If you said yes, are the ten subjects below boys' subjects or girls' subjects? Please tick.

	Boys	Girls	Neither
English			
Maths			
Science			
Art			
Geography			
History			
Modern Language			
Music			
PE			
Technology			

When you have all the responses back you can do the same exercise with your pupils, or with a group of them. For both adults and pupils it is interesting to look at the overall nature of response, and the response by gender. In a recent piece of research with nearly two hundred Year 7 pupils the outcomes in these two categories of information were as follows:

Are some school subjects boys' subjects or girls' subjects ?

	Yes	No	Unsure	No reply
Overall	29%	69%	1%	1%
Boys	28%	72%	1%	0%
Girls	29%	69%	0%	2%

(The percentages have been rounded up, and do not add up to 100%)

Pickering J (1996)

The figures point towards roughly two in three of the pupils saying they feel there are no differences between the subjects. The boy–girl responses were very close. How does that compare with your results ?

The one in three pupils who felt there were gender differences to subjects, 'divided up' the subjects into the following gender categories. Music and French were considered to be girls' subjects, whereas PE/Games and Technology were thought to be boys'. Science was not thought of as a boys' subject, although other studies have suggested this. English was not considered to be a girls' subject and Maths was not regarded as a boys' subject.

What did your findings show? Check for similarities and differences. Consider which findings surprise you and which do not.

Taking into account the responses of the adults and pupils consider if there are 'certainties' and 'confusions' about what constitutes a boys' subject and a girls' subject. If subjects have an under 20% rating as a 'gender' subject, then it is hard to argue that this perception is a widely held one, other than as a significant minority view. Can we, for instance, based on this evidence alone, argue that English is a girls' subject, other than in terms of what assessment outcomes seem to indicate?

Considering subject preference may suggest whether the assessment results differential can be explained by personal liking and whether it has a gender element in it. Take the same ten National Curriculum subjects, or give the pupils a free choice, and ask them to list up to four subjects which they like doing in school and up to four subjects which they dislike. Then add up all the figures and make percentages tables of the figures.

Look for both surprising and predictable outcomes, either on an overall basis or split by gender.

This is how the two hundred Year 7 pupils mentioned earlier responded:

Subject Likes	Overall	Boys	Girls
English	24%	23%	23%
PE/Games	20%	25%	16%
Art	13%	13%	13%
Maths	8%	15%	11%

Pickering J (1996)

There is no need to go into this information in detail. For our purposes linking personal likes to notions of gender and achievement reveal several key features:

(1)   *English is the most popular subject, and as many boys like it as girls.*
(2)   *More girls like Maths than boys.*
(3)   *French does not appear as a subject liked by girls.*

Subject Dislikes	Overall	Boys	Girls
French	31%	31%	31%
Humanities	15%	18%	12%
Maths	14%	16%	12%
Science	8%	7%	10%

Pickering J (1996)

How do your findings compare to these? Obviously most primary schools will not have the French result, but there may be similarities in the degree of dislike of particular areas.

As with the subject likes, there are interesting features in the dislike responses here:

(1) *French is equally disliked by boys and girls.*
(2) *English does not appear in the boys' dislikes.*
(3) *Maths is disliked by more boys than girls.*

Based on these figures there does not seem to be any real case for linking subject likes to examination or test performance. This group of pupils had reflected national patterns in their Key Stage 2 tests in the previous school year, with the boys over 10% below the girls in English and roughly the same in Maths and Science. Science, for instance, is not popular with boys or girls, but the KS2 test results were very good for this group of pupils. There also seems to be no justification for linking a liking for a subject with perceptions about its gender identity as indicated by the girls' attitude to French and PE/Games, and the boys to Technology.

However, it is important to bear in mind that this information is only a snapshot of what these pupils felt at that time, just as yours will reflect the current views of your pupils, although there may be a long-term link between the perceptions about a subject and liking for it over the eleven years which most children spend in school.

Despite this, do your results continue to show confusions and uncertainties? Or can you now see a pattern, which links clearly achievement to stereotypes about gender subjects and personal likes and dislikes? Perhaps it will be worth you returning to this at a later date to see if changes in attitudes to these two aspects can be linked to 'highs and lows' of progress in achievement .

2   Solution

It is hard to see what individual teachers can do in classrooms to influence the equitable nature of public tests and examinations. Given that there is probably no such thing as a fair test anyway, it would seem to be more profitable for teachers to do what they can to raise the achievement of all pupils, by working as effectively as possible within the current assessment context.

This brings us back to how teachers can best prepare their pupils to manage assessment challenges successfully. And it will come as no surprise that the key factor, in the eyes of pupils and professionals, is the way in which pupils are prepared by their teachers for these challenges. This applies to boys as much as to girls.

Stimulus Quotation 24

"The crucial factor in boys' attitudes towards English and their performance in the subject was the influence of the teacher ...When reading was taught well and pupils' private reading successfully encouraged, the distinctions between girls' and boys' reading interests were less sharp than usual ...
Boys' performance improved when they had a clear understanding of the progress they needed to make in order to achieve well ...In terms of their attitudes to the subject and performance in it, boys benefited when well-managed oral work was central to English."

Boys and English, *(OFSTED 1993)*

The successful encouragement and management of pupils' learning by an influential teacher return us to the theme which has run throughout the book. The interaction in schools between learner and teacher, based on clear targets set with and for pupils, is the single most significant factor in raising achievement.

In the minds of the pupils the issue of learning which leads to and beyond assessments is linked so closely to the quality of teaching it becomes the single key factor in effective learning. Indeed, it cannot be separated from the other issues this section has looked at, such as subject preference and stereotyping as causes of boys' underachievement.

Both assessment and subject preference may lead to boys' underachievement, but only if the poor quality of teaching makes them overriding issues. Where the quality of teacher–learner interactions is good, then other 'outside' factors slip away, to be replaced by the enjoyment and the challenge of the learning experience.

What do pupils themselves see as the key factors in teacher–learner interactions? And if the interactions are good, do they make a link between liking a subject and doing well in it?

Ask your pupils the following open-ended questions:

> What makes you like the subject/work you do in school?
>
> What makes you dislike the subject/work you do in school?
>
> Do you do better in subjects/work that you like than you do in subjects/work that you do not like? If you do, can you explain why? If you do not, can you explain why?

Research with the Year 7 pupils provided the following responses:

Liking the Subject	Overall	Boys	Girls
Good at the subject	6%	7%	4%
Subject interest	32%	30%	35%
Teaching factors	63%	64%	61%
Disliking the Subject	**Overall**	**Boys**	**Girls**
Not good at subject	5%	4%	5%
Subject issues	23%	20%	24%
Teaching factors	72%	74%	71%
Linking Likes to Performance **	**Overall**	**Boys**	**Girls**
Yes	86%	88%	85%
No	10%	8%	11%
Unsure	4%	3%	4%

** These pupils were not asked to explain their responses.

Pickering J (1996)

The similarity amongst the girls and boys on the links between liking subjects and standards of achievement was striking, and the overall linkage is as high as might be expected. Try the same survey with your pupils and see if the pattern of response is similar.

In the questions about subject likes and dislikes, the dominant aspect of teaching factors, which these pupils highlighted, showed an impressive consistency amongst boys and girls. In this sample they appear to reinforce the view that pupils are clear about what they feel would improve their learning, and it is linked inextricably with teachers and teaching. If you pick out the teaching factors from the answers that your pupils gave you about subject likes and dislikes, what are the major themes, and do they come across consistently? Most importantly, do they refer to specific teaching styles and strategies?

Research shows that boys appear to be more affected than girls by the absence of the teaching factors, but that all pupils respond positively and achieve well when these factors are present. Although one in 20 of all the pupils referred to not liking the teacher as a reason for disliking a subject, there was no specific reference to 'liking' the teacher as a reason for liking a subject.

There was certainly no reference to liking a teacher as an older friend, which is thought to be what some children – especially boys – want. Far from it in fact. The Year 11 boys in this school, who were interviewed as part of the study, said categorically that they reacted badly to teachers who tried to be too 'matey'. They wanted teachers who were friendly because they were approachable and human, and took a personal interest in

them as learners. They wanted their world understood and valued, but they did not want teachers to be part of it. One Year 11 boy went as far as to say that, if his teachers started wearing teenagers' clothes and talking about their music, he would probably start wearing Hush Puppies and do his clothes shopping at Dunn & Co! This research is supported by a study of Year 7 boys in an all-boys school.

Raising Boys' Achievement

Stimulus Quotation 25

"It was clear that their response to subjects was connected to the teacher, but not to whether they liked the teacher (although that might be an advantage). The critical factor appeared to be whether the teacher was effective. Among the things which they saw as important for effective learning, and which they relied upon the teacher to provide, were: keeping order; maintaining a good pace and level of demand; being clear about what was required; providing support and guidance for learning; having a warm relationship with pupils; providing opportunities for practical work; fairness."

Lodge C and Pickering J (1996)

In the end what pupils appear to be telling us is that teachers already have the solutions to problems about assessment and subject stereotyping. These solutions are based on what teachers do in their own classrooms. They may not agree with all or parts of the assessment procedures in school, but they can work within them to make pupils effective and efficient learners. This will be particularly helpful to many underachieving boys. Teachers may not find it easy to deal with the stereotypical attitudes of some boys – and girls – to certain subjects, but nearly all of them are 'biddable', if they are inspired to understand a learning process, that engages and involves them.

Case Study Six

Boutcher CE School, Southwark

This primary school was one of six involved in a study about reading and gender. The following report has been written by the independent researcher who carried out the research. It reminds us that schools can and do make a difference.

Early in 1996 a reading survey was carried out with Year 5 pupils in four primary schools and Year 7 pupils in two secondary schools in Southwark, a local education authority in south-east London. Over four hundred pupils were involved, of whom just over 250 completed questionnaires. I interviewed the remaining 150 pupils, including all 27 in Boutcher primary school.

The overall results showed predictable patterns in terms of gender differences, in reading and in differences between primary and secondary schools.

Gender Differences

Boys read more comics and newspapers, whereas girls read more books and magazines. More boys than girls read adventure books and about sport. Girls get their books from a wider range of sources than boys. Just over half of the boys play computer games every day, compared with less than one in five of the girls. Girls enjoy a wider range of books than boys. Girls' favourite type of reading is poetry; boys prefer information books. More boys than girls think they are good readers. Both boys and girls say that men and women read different sorts of things: men read newspapers, sport and action and adventure books while women read magazines, romance and long books.

Primary and Secondary Schools

Secondary school pupils read fewer books, but more newspapers and magazines. They also read about double the amount of non-fiction. Primary school pupils read a wider range of fiction and choose their books from a wider variety of sources, except the public library. Secondary school pupils watch considerably more television. There is a decline of nearly a quarter of the types of books enjoyed by secondary school pupils, as well as a drop of a third in the enjoyment of various reading activities. Fewer secondary school pupils think that they will read books when they have left school.

General Findings

The aggregated data for all six schools provided useful baseline data about reading habits and attitudes. However, it was interesting to see that there was a huge variation from school to school, which was not revealed by the overall figures. This variation was apparent when the information was looked at by gender and by ethnicity. But it was far more marked when looked at by simply comparing school to school. School differences were more apparent throughout the findings on reading. They were less so in some aspects of watching television, an area over which schools have little or no influence.

These findings suggested that schools can make a significant difference in influencing reading frequency, variety and enjoyment. Where schools' literacy provision and teacher commitment were overt and plentiful, there was far more reading by pupils and far more enthusiasm about books.

The Primary School

The data collected from the interviews with the pupils in Boutcher school makes interesting reading on its own, standing out as it does from the other five schools in the survey. It showed that, in this particular school, the level of reading overall was very high and that the boys figured prominently in this. BUT, what stood out, almost from the moment that I walked into the classroom, were three key factors in explaining the figures.

First, the room was an immensely stimulating reading environment. The books were prominently and attractively displayed, with a wide variety of fiction and non-fiction on show. There were book corners and there were books of all sorts close to where all children worked.

Second, the children had a passion for books. I was almost overwhelmed by children wanting to talk to me about their reading. They showed me their reading folders, they offered to read to me, individually and in groups, and they wanted me to read to them, individually and in groups.

Third, the teacher had a clear commitment to and love of books. From the moment the morning began with a reading of a poem, through group reading, topic work, some science exploration and on to the class story at the end of the day, there was a feel for the value and pleasure of books, which came overtly from the way the teacher used and spoke of books.

And what precisely did the results of the interviews show? Whilst remembering that the overall figures for both boys and girls were much higher than the other five schools, the boys in this school 'scored' consistently higher than the girls in most aspects of reading. They read more books, comics and newspapers for pleasure; they read as much fiction as the girls; they got their books from a wider range of sources; they liked poetry more than girls; they enjoyed a far larger variety of reading activities, including writing about reading; they valued good expression in readers equally with girls; and they saw themselves more likely to be reading fiction and non-fiction books when they left school.

It was not all non-stereotypical response. The boys still enjoyed fun in books as opposed to good characters, which the girls liked. And, even though all the boys wanted to improve their reading, they had no real idea how to do it, compared with the girls, who suggested plenty of strategies.

What the data also revealed was the fact that over half the boys thought that men and women read similar kinds of books. This compared with nearly three quarters of the boys in the other schools who thought men and women read different kinds of books. Given what the boys read on their own, in groups of boys, in groups of boys and girls, and to me that day, all with no apparent regard for the gender acceptability of the books, I can only hope that they pass this love for all reading on to their offspring, when the time comes!

Raising Boys' Achievement

(Do's and Don'ts) (Before moving on)

Don't confuse boys' attitudes with approaches to learning $\longrightarrow$	Do look to what makes individual boys effective learners
Don't assume peer group pressure works in a blanket way $\longrightarrow$	Do look at what makes many boys successful and respected learners
Don't think that teachers cannot affect boys' dispositions to learning $\longrightarrow$	Do support and develop boys' and girls' learning strategies
Don't think that a female world is bad for boys' education $\longrightarrow$	Do try to treat all pupils fairly regardless of how they present themselves
Don't tell boys what might be best for them in the long run $\longrightarrow$	Do work with boys on target setting and action planning
Don't think that boys will come good in examinations $\longrightarrow$	Do accept that boys in particular are sensitive to teachers and effective teaching

Going Back and Looking Forward

At the start six claims were made about how this book could help teachers and schools to raise boys' achievement. The conclusion gives you a checklist to use to see if the book has helped you develop your ideas about boys' underachievement.

It is unlikely that all of the book will have been useful, and some parts may have been more successful than others, hopefully giving you new insights or refining current ideas and strategies. But, in the search to raise standards of achievement in schools in different settings, the sharing of a wide range of possible strategies should provide continued ideas about the learning of our children.

After you have run through the checklist, you will be offered six ways to help extend your thinking and practice in relation to underachieving boys in particular and all pupils in general.

Back to the Beginning

Reflect on what you have read in this book and the activities which you have been able to undertake in your school(s). Then go through the checklist and its stimulus questions to see if you are now more informed and confident about how to work on improving the achievement of boys.

1   **Making generalisations about boys**
   ● Can it be done, nationally or in your school?
   ● How do the boys in your classroom/school benefit from any generalisations which you can make?

2   **Focusing on boys in classrooms**
   ● What causes of boys' underachievement did you find with your boys?
   ● Were these the same as your original thoughts?
   ● How do your findings compare with other colleagues' thoughts?
   ● How many solutions to your boys' underachievement did you come up with?

3   **Involving boys in discussions about underachievement**
   ● Did you find this difficult?
   ● Did you find this profitable? If so, in what ways and to what end?
   ● If not, what happened to make the exchange unprofitable?
   ● Did the boys find this difficult?
   ● Did they find it profitable? If so, in what ways and to what end?
     If not, what happened to make the exchange unprofitable?

4   **Looking at exemplars of work with boys in other schools**
   ● Were any of the case studies helpful? If so, how?
   ● Are there any strategies in the case studies which you might use in your own school?
   ● Has your school(s) got strategies which might work in other schools?
     If so, have you been able to share them? If not, would you like to ?
   ● Do you belong to a local or national network for the exchange of ideas?

5   **Extra resourcing**
   - If you tried some or all of the activities, how much time and energy did it take up?
   - How much extra time/money did you get? How much did you need?
   - How much time/money would be needed for you to work with boys even more effectively?
   - If you were unable to do some or all of the activities, were resources of time and money a problem? If so, how much do you need? How much, realistically, can you have?

6   **There is no 'quick fix' !**
   - Were there some things which you were able to fix quickly, which have led to better achievement by boys, individually or in groups?
   - Which long-term strategies look like working with underachieving boys? What are the predicted outcomes for the boys?
   - How are you planning to develop strategies for raising boys' achievement?
   - Can you see differences in the attitudes to learning of many pupils, not just underachieving boys? If so, can you explain this, in terms of 'feel' and/or 'hard data'?

Looking forward: Six Suggestions for Developing Work with Boys – and Girls!

1   **Using pupils as co-researchers about learning**

Stimulus Quotation 26

"... action research with students as key participants had the immediate impact of applying research to classroom practice. Students were not only recipients of these findings but generators of knowledge."

from **The Educational Forum,** *Vol.57 Summer, SooHoo S (Phi Delta Kappan, 1993)*

If you have not done so already, it is worth trying to set some pupils off on their own research project. But it should be about issues of learning, teaching and curriculum, not just the traditional 'comfort' issues of the environment, uniform and catering. For this to happen you will need to be sure that you are prepared to ...

2   **... Use pupils as indispensable resources in discussions about their learning**
Even when teachers work with pupils to discuss learning needs, strategies and outcomes, there can be a temptation to regard the pupils as the less important member of the partnership. This is linked usually to the age and lack of maturity which we feel may characterise children. To do so is unwise, because it provides any pupil–teacher dialogue with less information than may otherwise be forthcoming from the very people who have more of a vested interest than us in the outcome.

What children say to us can tell us so much about our business.

> **Stimulus Quotation 27**
>
> "... educators have forgotten the important connection between teachers and students. We listen to outside experts to inform us, and, consequently, we overlook the treasure in our own backyards: our students. Student perceptions are valuable to our practice because they are authentic sources: they personally experience our classrooms firsthand. As teachers, we need to find ways to continually seek out these silent voices because they can teach us so much about learning and learners."
>
> from **The Educational Forum,** *Vol.57 Summer, SooHoo S (Phi Delta Kappan, 1993)*

3   Be prepared to 'dig deep' with pupils about their learning

There is a danger that teachers may go overboard when it comes to involving pupils in discussions about raising achievement. Try not to take an over-romanticised view of the work you do, because pupils are just one of the resources schools have to provide an active feedback loop about how learning is going. But you may have to accept that any shallow or irregular discussions with pupils will not provide the in-depth insights you want, and they may backfire if the pupils feel they are being used or patronised. But not digging deep with pupils about learning runs the risk of school-based change being ill-conceived.

> **Stimulus Quotation 28**
>
> "... educational transformation cannot take place without the inclusion of the voices of students, among others in the dialogue."
>
> from **Harvard Educational Review,** *Vol.64, Nieto S (1994)*

4   Trust pupils to work maturely and responsibly with you on their learning

Trust is an underused word in schools. This is partly because schools are seen commonly as adversarial places – the 'them and us' syndrome. This applies particularly to the learner-teacher relationship. As a result pupils are seen all too often as not worthy of trust, and are treated consequently as the untrustworthy, with little regard for the levels of trust which they are accorded outside school. This may be reinforced also by teachers' understandable worries that, if they trust pupils to talk about their learning, they may then say unkind things about the teaching. And no-one wants to have too much of that! But most of the research evidence shows that what pupils and teachers want in schools are remarkably similar, and that these pupils, particularly the less effective learners, are mature and responsible enough to join with teachers to explore learning.

Stimulus Quotation 29

"... it is our view that the conditions of learning that prevail in the majority of our secondary schools do not adequately take account of the maturity of young people, nor of the tensions and pressures that they experience as they struggle to reconcile the demands of their social and personal development with the development of their identities as learners. Out of school ... they carry quite tough responsibilities, balancing multiple roles and often finding themselves dealing with conflicting loyalties ... In contrast, the structures of secondary schooling offer, on the whole, less responsibility and autonomy than many young people are accustomed to in their lives outside school, and less opportunities for learning-related tensions to be explored."

School Improvement: What Can Pupils Tell Us? *Rudduck J, Chaplain R and Wallace G (David Fulton, 1996)*

5   Schools need to develop learners for life

This is not just the argument about the importance of understanding and learning about learning, so that all the assessment hoops can be jumped through successfully. This is very important, but it is not all that pupils need to learn. Professor Michael Barber's book, *The Learning Game* (Gollancz, 1996), gives fascinating insights into why an education revolution is needed. He argues that an individual learning promise is required for all children, and that much of this is necessary so that the children of today can become the citizens of tomorrow. They need to be equipped in terms of their learning achievements and potential to deal with many of the problems which the citizens of the late twentieth century will have bequeathed them. To do this pupils need to be enabled, and then empowered to talk about their learning.

Stimulus Quotation 30

"Empowering students is not so much concerned with neutralising their dissent as allowing them to feel able to explore, experiment, to learn to argue and to negotiate within the sheltered environment of the school classroom, the peer group, the school council."

Sharing Power in Schools, *Trafford B (Derbyshire, Education Now,1993)*

6   Let pupils know we support their learning

If there is to be a real learner–teacher partnership about learning, then teachers have to stand full square behind their pupils. This is not always easy to do with all pupils, particularly some of the boys in your classrooms. Perhaps your first step way back at the beginning of the book should have been to ask pupils whether they feel supported by their teachers, their schools, society at large. The answer would probably have been no, or, at best, a very qualified yes.

Supporting them does not necessarily mean praising them where praise is not due. It means persuading them that we will do our best to challenge the view, when it is offered, that ...

Stimulus Quotation 31

"The baggy jeans, shaven-headed, baseball-capped with no brains or moral stereotype is becoming increasingly accepted. Boys are now being labelled as irresponsible, lazy, unambitious thugs whose only desires in life are to take drugs and steal cars."

from 'A' Level Essays, Hitchin Boys' School, Fitzpatrick S, (1995)

This comment about how adults perceive boys comes from an achieving boy, one of the many in our schools.

A classmate of his, another achieving boy, offers a fitting end note to this book. It is simple, and a good topic for debate at any staff meeting – and with pupils, especially boys.

Stimulus Quotation 32

"School should be a place that inspires learning"

from 'A' Level Essays, Hitchin Boys' School, Pattar T, (1995)

References

Recommended Reading and Useful Contacts

Barton A — Words of Comfort for Males. Boys are under-achieving. What can we do? *Times Educational Supplement*, (22/03/1996) © Times Supplement Ltd (1997)

Barber M — *Young People and their Attitudes to School*. An interim report of a research project in the Centre for Successful Schools, Keele University (1994)

Barber M — *The Learning Game*. Gollancz (1996)

Barrs M and Pidgeon S (eds.) — *Reading the Difference*. London: CLPE (1993)

Benskin F — *Black Children and Underachievement in Schools*. London: Minerva Press (1994)

Bradford W — *Raising Boys' Achievement*. Primary and Secondary Versions. Kirklees Education (1996)

Broadfoot P, James M, McMeeking P, Nuttall D and Stierer B — *Records of Achievement – Report of the National Evaluation of Pilot Schemes*. London: HMSO (1988)

Cenre for Language in Primary Education — *Webber Row, London. SE1 8QW*

City of Westminster Education and Leisure — *Working with Very Able Children*. London (1996)

Connell R W — Cool Guys, Swots and Wimps: the Interplay of Masculinity & Education. *Oxford Review of Education* Vol. 15, No.3 (1989)

Cullingford C — *The Inner World of the School*. London: Cassell (1991)

DfEE — *Code of Practice on the Identification and Assessment of Special Educational Needs*. DfEE, London (1994)

Elwood J and Comber C — *Gender Differences in 'A' level Examinations: the Reinforcements of Stereotypes?* Paper presented to ECER Conference, Bath (1995)

Fitzpatrick S and Pattar T — from 'A' level essays written at Hitchin Boys' School, Hertfordshire (1995)

Gender and Education — Dept. of Continuing Education, University of Warwick, Coventry. CV4 7AL

| Grant L | Under Pressure © *The Guardian* (11/03/1996) |

Hannan G — *Improving Boys' Performance.* INSET materials. (1996) Bank Cottage, Bourton Road, Much Wenlock, Shropshire TF13 6AJ. Tel: 01952 727332

Harris S, Nixon J, and Rudduck J — School Work, Homework and Gender. *Gender and Education,* Vol. 5, No. 1, pp. 3-15 Carfax (1993)

John G — View from the Front Line. © *The Guardian.* (26/09/1995)

Jordan E — Fighting Boys and Fantasy Play: the Construction of Masculinity in the Early Years of the School. *Gender and Education,* Vol. 7, No. 1, pp. 69-83 Carfax (1995)

La France M — School for Scandal: Differential Experiences for Females and Males. *Gender and Education,* Vol. 3, No. 1, pp. 3-15 Carfax (1987)

Lodge C and Pickering J — *Boys' Underachievement: Challenging Some Assumptions.* Paper presented to BERA Conference, Lancaster (1996)

Louis, K S and Miles M — *Improving the Urban High School.* London: Cassell (1990)

Mac an Ghaill M — *The Making of Men.* Buckingham: OUP (1994)

Mahoney P — *Schools for the Boys?* London: Hutchinson (1985)

Nieto S — Lessons from Students in Creating a Chance to Dream. *Harvard Educational Review,* Vol. 64, pp. 392-426 (1994)

OFSTED — Boys and English (1993)

O'Leary J and Charter D — Anti-School bias 'blights boys for life'. (06/03/1996) *The Times* © Times Newspapers Ltd 1996

Parry O — What's Sex Got To Do With It? *The Guardian* (05/09/1996)

Phelan P, Cao H and Davidson L — Speaking Up: Students' Perspectives on School. *Phi Delta Kappan,* Vol. 73, No. 9, pp 695–704 (1992)

Pickering J — Involving Pupils in School Improvement. *Research Matters* Vol. 6. London: Institute of Education (1997)

Riddell S — *Politics and the Gender of the Curriculum.* London: Routledge (1992)

Rudduck J, Chaplain, R and Wallace G — *School Improvement: What Can Pupils Tell Us?* London: David Fulton (1995)

Salisbury J and Jackson D — *Challenging Macho Values.* London: Falmer Press (1996)

SCAA — *Boys and English.* London: SCAA (1996)

SOED — *Using Ethos Indicators in School Self Evaluation.* Edinburgh: SOED (1992)

Sewell T   *Black Masculinities and Schooling.* London: Trentham
                                Press (1997)

SooHoo S   Students as Partners in Research and
                                Restructuring Schools. *The Educational Forum*, Vol. 57,
                                Summer, pp. 386–393 *Phi Delta Kappan* (1993)

Stoll L and Fink D   *Changing Our Schools.* Buckingham: Open University (1996)

Times Educational   Not Working (15/03/1996) © *Times Supplements Ltd* (1997)
Supplement

Trafford B   *Sharing Power in Schools.* Derbyshire: Education Now (1993)

Warrington M   *Differential Achievement of Girls and Boys at GCSE.*
and Younger M   Cambridge: Homerton College (1995)

Weis L   *Working Class Without Work.* London: Routledge (1990)

INDEX

Fitzpatrick S, 97
French, 84, 85, 86

G

GCSEs, 31, 50, 79, 80, 81
gender identity, 37–43, 50, *see also* peer
  group pressure; role models
genetic make-up, 47, 48
girl-friendly teaching methods, 29, 50
girls,
  boys attitudes to, 38, 42
  raising achievement, 67
  traditional ambitions, 67
girls' activities/subjects, 50, 58, 77, 83–9
good practice, *see* sharing good practice

H

handwriting, 77
Hannan G, 50, 53, 65–6
  Improving Boys' Performance, 33, 48, 51,
  52
Harris S, Nixon, J and Rudduck J, *Gender
  and Education*, 67
Hartcliffe School, Bristol, 54
Hitchin Boys' School, Hertfordshire, 44, 97
Hodgeon J, *Reading the Difference*, 57, 64
home/social background, 49
Homerton College, Cambridge, 32, 33
homework, 27, 40, 72, 77
Honey P and Mumford A, *The Manual of
  Learning Styles*, 34

I

individual learning needs, assessing,
  16–19, 26, 73–5, 96
  Individual Education Plans, 17, 19, 73,
  75
individuals, treating boys as, 7, 45, 50, 70,
  75, 92
INSET, 8, 65, 66
Institute of Education, London, 32
interviewing boys, 31, 33, 38
involving boys, 7, 19, 22–3, 27, 35, 66, 93,
  94

J

Job opportunities, *see* employment
  opportunities
John G, *View from the Front Line*, 58
Jordan E, *Gender and Education*, 38, 42

K

Keele University, 31, 32
Key Stage assessments, *see* assessment

L

La France, M, 59–63
laddish behaviour, 37, 70
learning needs, *see* individual learning
  needs
learning styles, 29, 34, 48, 50, 53, 79
  boys', 31, 34, 44, 47, 53
  girls', 47–8, 80
LEA-school partnership, 76–8
linguistic intelligence, 47, 48
Louis K S and Miles M, *Improving the
  Urban High School*, 21

M

MacBeath J, 32
males
  as authority figures, 64
  dominance of, 67, 70
  as mentors, 58
  as role models, 27, 29, 57
  as teachers, 63
  traditional roles of, 41, 42
Maths, 71, 76, 77, 85, 86
media perceptions of boys, 7, 11, 12
mentoring programme, 58
Minns H, *Reading the Difference*, 49
mixed-sex schools, 8
monitoring, 16, 19, 73
motivation, 21, 33, 35, 36, 72, 75
Music, 84

Other Titles from Network Educational Press

THE SCHOOL EFFECTIVENESS SERIES

Raising Boys' Achievement is the sixth title in The School Effectiveness Series, which focuses on practical and useful ideas for school teachers. This series addresses the issues of whole school improvement along with new knowledge about teaching and learning, and offers straightforward solutions which teachers can use to make life more rewarding for themselves and those they teach.

Book 1: *Accelerated Learning in the Classroom* by Alistair Smith

- The first book in the UK to apply new knowledge about the brain to classroom practice
- Contains practical methods so teachers can apply accelerated learning theories to their own classrooms
- Aims to increase the pace of learning and deepen understanding
- Includes advice on how to create the ideal environment for learning and how to help learners fulfil their potential
- Full of lively illustrations, diagrams and plans
- Offers practical solutions on improving performance, motivation and understanding
- Contains a checklist of action points for the classroom – 21 ways to improve learning

Book 2: *Effective Learning Activities* by Chris Dickinson

- An essential teaching guide which focuses on practical activities to improve learning
- Aims to improve results through effective learning, which will raise achievement, deepen understanding, promote self-esteem and improve motivation
- Includes activities which are designed to promote differentiation and understanding
- Offers advice on how to maximise the use of available – and limited – resources
- Includes activities suitable for GCSE, National Curriculum, Highers, GSVQ and GNVQ
- From the author of the highly acclaimed 'Differentiation: A Practical Handbook of Classroom Strategies'

Book 3: *Effective Heads of Department* by Phil Jones & Nick Sparks

- An ideal support for Heads of Department looking to develop necessary management skills
- Contains a range of practical systems and approaches; each of the eight sections ends with a 'checklist for action'
- Designed to develop practice in line with OFSTED expectations and DfEE thinking by monitoring and improving quality
- Addresses issues such as managing resources, leadership, learning, departmental planning and making assessment valuable
- Includes useful information for Senior Managers in schools who are looking to enhance the effectiveness of their Heads of Department

Book 4: *Lessons are for Learning* by Mike Hughes

- Brings together the theory of learning with the realities of the classroom environment
- Encourages teachers to reflect on their own classroom practice and challenges them to think about why they teach in the way they do
- Develops a clear picture of what constitutes effective classroom practice
- Offers practical suggestions for activities that bridge the gap between recent developments in the theory of learning and the constraints of classroom teaching
- Ideal for stimulating thought and generating discussion
- Written by a practising teacher who has also worked as a teaching advisor, a PGCE co-ordinator and an OFSTED inspector

Book 5: *Effective Learning in Science* by Paul Denley and Keith Bishop
- Looks at planning for effective learning within the context of science
- Encourages discussion about the aims and purposes in teaching science and the role of subject knowledge in effective teaching
- Tackles issues such as planning for effective learning, the use of resources and other relevant management issues
- Offers help in the development of a departmental plan to revise schemes of work, resources and classroom strategies, in order to make learning and teaching more effective
- Ideal for any science department aiming to increase performance and improve results

Book 7: *Effective Provision for Able & Talented Children* by Barry Teare
- Basic theory, necessary procedures and turning theory into practice
- Main methods of identifying the able and talented
- Concerns about achievement and appropriate strategies to raise achievement
- The role of the classroom teacher, monitoring and evaluation techniques
- Practical enrichment activities and appropriate resources

Book 8: *Effective Careers Education & Guidance* by Andrew Edwards and Anthony Barnes
- Strategic planning of the careers programme as part of the wider curriculum
- Practical consideration of managing careers education and guidance
- Practical activities for reflection and personal learning, and case studies where such activities have been used
- Aspects of guidance and counselling involved in helping students to understand their own capabilities and form career plans
- Strategies for reviewing and developing existing practice

Book 9: *Best behaviour and Best behaviour FIRST AID* by
Peter Relf, Rod Hirst, Jan Richardson and Georgina Youdell
- Provides support for those who seek starting points for effective behaviour management, for individual teachers and for middle and senior managers
- Focuses on practical and useful ideas for individual schools and teachers

Best behaviour FIRST AID
(pack of 5 booklets)
- Provides strategies to cope with aggression, defiance and disturbance
- Straightforward action points for self-esteem

Book 10: *The Effective School Governor* by David Marriott
(including free audio tape)
- Straightforward guidance on how to fulfil a governor's role and responsibilities
- Develops your personal effectiveness as an individual governor
- Practical support on how to be an effective member of the governing team
- Audio tape for use in car or at home

Book 11: *Improving Personal Effectiveness for Managers in Schools* by James Johnson
- An invaluable resource for new and experienced teachers in both primary and secondary schools
- Contains practical strategies for improving leadership and management skills
- Focuses on self-management skills, managing difficult situations, working under pressure, developing confidence, creating a team ethos and communicating effectively

Book 12: *Making Pupil Data Powerful* by Maggie Pringle and Tony Cobb
- Shows teachers in primary, middle and secondary schools how to interpret pupils' performance data and how to use it to enhance teaching and learning
- Provides practical advice on analysing performance and learning behaviours, measuring progress, predicting future attainment, setting targets and ensuring continuity and progression
- Explains how to interpret national initiatives on data-analysis, benchmarking and target-setting, and to ensure that these have value in the classroom

Book 13: *Closing the Learning Gap* by Mike Hughes
- Helps teachers, departments and schools to close the Learning Gap between what we know about effective learning and what actually goes on in the classroom
- Encourages teachers to reflect on the ways in which they teach, and to identify and implement strategies for improving their practice
- Helps teachers to apply recent research findings about the brain and learning
- Full of practical advice and real, tested strategies for improvement
- Written by a teacher, for teachers, to stimulate thought and interest 'at a glance'

Book 14: *Getting Started* by Henry Leibling
- Provides invaluable advice for Newly Qualified Teachers (NQTs) during the three-term induction period that comprises their first year of teaching.
- Advice includes strategies on how to get to know the school and the new pupils, how to work with induction tutors, and when to ask for help.

Book 15: *Leading the Learning School* by Colin Weatherley
The main theme is that the effective leadership of true 'learning schools' involves applying the principles of learning to all levels of educational management:
- Learning – 13 key principles of learning are derived from a survey of up-to-date knowledge of the brain and learning
- Teaching – how to use the key principles of learning to improve teachers' professional knowledge and skills, make the learning environment more supportive and improve the design of learning activities
- Staff Development – how the same principles that should underpin the design and teaching of learning activities for pupils should underpin the design and provision of development activities for teachers
- Organizational Development – how a learning school should be consciously managed according to these same key principles of learning. The section proposes a radical new 'whole brain' approach to Development Planning

Book 16: *Adventures in Learning* by Mike Tilling
- Integrate other theories about how we learn into a coherent 'vision' of learning that unfolds over time
- Recognise the phases of the Learner's Journey and make practical interventions at key moments
- Shape the experience of learners from the 'micro' level of the individual lesson to the 'macro' level of the learning lifetime

Book 17: *Strategies for Closing the Learning Gap* by Mike Hughes with Andy Vass
- Highlights and simplifies key issues emerging from the latest discoveries about how the human brain learns
- Offers proven, practical strategies and suggestions as to how to apply this new research in the classroom, to improve students' learning and help them achieve their full potential
- Written and arranged in the same easy-to-read style as *Closing the Learning Gap*, to encourage teachers to browse through it during 'spare' moments

Book 18: *Classroom Management* by Philip Waterhouse and Chris Dickinson
- Classic best-selling text by Philip Waterhouse, set in the current context by Chris Dickinson
- Full of practical ideas to help teachers find ways of integrating Key Skills and Thinking Skills into an already overcrowded curriculum
- Shows how Induction Standards, OFSTED requirements and the findings of the Hay McBer report into School Effectiveness can be met or implemented through carefully thought out strategies for the management and organisation of the classroom
- Covers topics including whole-class presentation, dialogue and interactive teaching; teacher-led small group work; classroom layout; interpersonal relationships in the classroom; and collaborative teamwork

ACCELERATED LEARNING SERIES
General Editor: **Alistair Smith**

Accelerated Learning in Practice by Alistair Smith
- The author's second book, which takes Nobel Prize winning brain research into the classroom.
- Structured to help readers access and retain the information necessary to begin to accelerate their own learning and that of the students they teach.
- Contains over 100 learning tools, case studies from 36 schools and an up-to-the-minute resource section
- Includes nine principles of learning based on brain research and the author's seven-stage Accelerated Learning Cycle.

The ALPS Approach: Accelerated Learning in Primary Schools
by Alistair Smith and Nicola Call
- Shows how research on how we learn, collected by Alistair Smith, can be used to great effect in the primary classroom.
- Provides practical and accessible examples of strategies used by highly experienced primary teacher Nicola Call, at a school where the SATs results shot up as a consequence.
- Professional, practical and exhilarating resource that gives readers the opportunity to develop the ALPS approach for themselves and for the children in their care.
- The ALPS approach includes: Exceeding expectation, 'Can-do' learning, Positive performance, Target-setting that works, Using review for recall, Preparing for tests ... and much more.

MapWise by Oliver Caviglioli and Ian Harris
- Provides informed access to the most powerful accelerated learning technique around – Model Mapping.
- Shows how mapping can be used to address National Curriculum thinking skills requirements for students of any preferred learning style by infusing thinking into subject teaching.
- Describes how mapping can be used to measure and develop intelligence.
- Explains how mapping supports teacher explanation and student understanding.
- Demonstrates how mapping makes planning, teaching and reviewing easier and more effective.
- Written and illustrated to be lively and engaging, practical and supportive.

The ALPS Resource Book by Alistair Smith and Nicola Call
- Follow-up to the authors' best-selling book *The ALPS Approach*, structured carefully to extend the theoretical and practical advice given in that publication.
- Provides a wealth of photocopiable, 'hands-on' resources for teachers to use in, and outside, the classroom.
- Describes over 1000 useful ideas for teachers to 'accelerate' children's learning, including affirmation posters for your classroom; how to make target-setting easy, fun and useful; rules and guidelines for positive behaviour; writing frames and thinking skills templates; how to help children better understand their brain and get it to work; advice on managing attention and dealing with groups; ten ways to improve test performance; sample school policies; 101 'brain break' activities that connect to learning.

Bright Sparks: Motivational posters for pupils by Alistair Smith
Over 100 photocopiable posters to help motivate pupils and help improve their learning.

- The magic spelling strategy
- How you learn best
- The abc of motivation
- Exam technique

Leading Learning: Staff development posters for schools by Alistair Smith
With over 200 posters which draw from the best in brain research from around the world.

- 5 features of learning to learn
- Smart marking
- Target setting
- Thinking skills

Creating An Accelerated Learning School by Derek Wise and Mark Lovatt
- Successfully using the learning cycle as a planning tool
- Providing planning time within the school week for teachers to plan and review together
- Using ICT to underpin the initiative
- Supporting staff in the classroom with 'learning coaches'
- Establishing a Learning to Learn course for all new students to give them the tools and skills they will need to fully engage in the learning process
- Producing its own training materials: handbook, planners, bulletins
- Careful and through recruitment and induction of new staff
- Aligning planning, monitoring and performance management to focus on the learning process.

EDUCATION PERSONNEL MANAGEMENT SERIES
These new Education Personnel Management handbooks will help headteachers, senior managers and governors to manage a broad range of personnel issues.

The Well Teacher – management strategies for beating stress, promoting staff health and reducing absence
by Maureen Cooper
- Provides straightforward, practical advice on how to deal strategically with staff absenteeism, which can be so expensive in terms of sick pay and supply cover, through proactively promoting staff health.
- Includes suggestions for reducing stress levels in schools.
- Outlines ways in which to deal with individual cases of staff absence.

Managing Challenging People – dealing with staff conduct
by Bev Curtis and Maureen Cooper
- Deals with managing staff whose conduct gives cause for concern.
- Summarises the employment relationship in schools, as well as those areas of education and employment law relevant to staff discipline.
- Looks at the differences between conduct and capability, and between misconduct and gross misconduct.
- Describes disciplinary and dismissal procedures relating to teaching and non-teaching staff, including headteachers.
- Describes case studies and model procedures, and provides pro-forma letters to help schools with these difficult issues.

Managing Poor Performance – handling staff capability issues
by Bev Curtis and Maureen Cooper
- Explains clearly why capability is important in providing an effective and high quality education for pupils.
- Gives advice on how to identify staff with poor performance, and how to help them improve.
- Outlines the legal position and the role of governors in dealing with the difficult issues surrounding poor performance.
- Details the various stages of formal capability procedures and dismissal hearings.
- Describes case studies and model procedures, and provides pro-forma letters.

Managing Allegations Against Staff – personnel and child protection issues in schools
by Maureen Cooper
- Provides invaluable advice to headteachers, senior managers and personnel staff on how to deal with the difficult issues arising from accusations made against school employees.
- Shows what schools can do to protect students, while safeguarding employees from the potentially devastating consequences of false allegations.
- Describes real-life case studies.
- Provides a clear outline of the legal background plus a moral code of conduct for staff.

Managing Recruitment and Selection – appointing the best staff
by Bev Curtis and Maureen Cooper
- Guides schools through the legal minefield of anti-discrimination, human rights and other legislation relevant when making appointments.
- Provides senior managers and staffing committees with help in many areas, including developing effective selection procedures, creating job descriptions and personnel specifications, writing better job advertisements and short-listing and interviewing techniques.

Managing Redundancies – dealing with reduction and reorganisation of staff
by Bev Curtis and Maureen Cooper
- Provides guidance in how to handle fairly and carefully the unsettling and sensitive issue of making staff redundant.
- Gives independent advice on keeping staff informed of their options, employment and other relevant legislation, sources of support (including the LEA) and working to the required time-scales.

VISIONS OF EDUCATION SERIES

The Unfinished Revolution by John Abbott and Terry Ryan
- Draws on evidence from the past to show how shifting attitudes in society and politics have shaped Western education systems.
- Argues that what is now needed is a completely fresh approach, designed around evidence about how children actually learn.
- Describes a vision of an education system based on current research into how our brains work, and designed to encourage the autonomous and inventive thinkers and learners that the 21st century demands.
- Essential reading for anyone involved in education and policy making.

The Child is Father of the Man by John Abbott
Also from one of the authors of 'The Unfinished Revolution'. The book outlines how his ideas about schools, thinking, learning and teaching have developed.

The Learning Revolution by Jeannette Vos and Gordon Dryden
The book includes a huge wealth of data and research from around the world.
- The 16 main trends to shape tomorrow's world
- The 13 steps to create a learning society
- The 20 steps to teach yourself anything you need
- The 12 steps to transform an education system
- How to change the way the world learns

Wise Up by Guy Claxton
The book teaches us how to raise children who are curious and confident explorers, and how we ourselves can learn to pair problem-solving with creativity. This is essential and compelling reading for parents, educators and managers alike.

THE LITERACY COLLECTION

Helping With Reading by Anne Butterworth and Angela White
- Includes sections on 'Hearing Children Read', Word Recognition' and 'Phonics'.
- Provides precisely focused, easily implemented follow-up activities for pupils who need extra reinforcement of basic reading skills.
- Provides clear, practical and easily implemented activities that directly relate to the National Curriculum and 'Literacy Hour' group work. Ideas and activities can also be incorporated into Individual Education Plans.
- Aims to address current concerns about reading standards and to provide support for classroom assistants and parents helping with the teaching of reading.

Class Talk by Rosemary Sage
- Looks at teacher–student communication and reflects on what is happening in the classroom.
- Looks at how students talk in different classroom situations and evaluates this information in terms of planning children's learning.
- Considers the problems of transmitting meaning to others.
- Discusses and reflects on practical strategies to improve the quality of talking, teaching and learning.

PRACTICAL RESOURCE BOOKS

Effective Resources for Able and Talented Children by Barry Teare
- A practical sequel to Barry Teare's Effective Provision for Able and Talented Children (see above), which can nevertheless be used entirely independently.
- Contains a wealth of photocopiable resources for able and talented pupils in both the primary and secondary sectors.
- Provides activities designed to inspire, motivate, challenge and stretch able children, encouraging them to enjoy their true potential.
- Resources are organised into National Curriculum areas, such as Literacy, Science and Humanities, each preceded by a commentary outlining key principles and giving general guidance for teachers.

More Effective Resources for Able and Talented Children by Barry Teare
- A treasury of stimulating and challenging activities to provide excitement and enrichment for more able children of all ages.
- can be used in situations both within and beyond normal classroom lessons, including differentiated homework, summer schools, clubs and competitions.
- All activities are photocopiable and accompanied by comprehensive solutions and notes for teachers.
- Resources are divided into several themes: English and literacy; mathematics and numeracy; science; humanities, citizenship, problem solving, decision making and information processing; modern foreign languages; young children; logical thought; detective work and codes; lateral thinking; competitions.

Imagine That... by Stephen Bowkett
- Hands-on, user-friendly manual for stimulating creative thinking, talking and writing in the classroom.
- Provides over 100 practical and immediately useable classroom activities and games that can be used in isolation, or in combination, to help meet the requirements and standards of the National Curriculum.
- Explores the nature of creative thinking and how this can be effectively driven through an ethos of positive encouragement, mutual support and celebration of success and achievement.
- Empowers children to learn how to learn.

Self-Intelligence by Stephen Bowkett
- Helps explore and develop emotional resourcefulness in teachers and their pupils.
- Aims to help teachers and pupils develop the high-esteem that underpins success in education.